SANDOWN PUBLIC LIBRARY
305 MAIN STREET · P.O. BOX
SANDOWN, NH 03873

W9-AQJ-785

DEEP DRIVE

DEEP DRIVE

A LONG JOURNEY TO FINDING THE CHAMPION WITHIN

World Series MVP

MIKE LOWELL

with Rob Bradford

With a Foreword by Josh Beckett

A CELEBRA BOOK

Celebra
Published by New American Library, a division of
Penguin Group (USA) Inc., 375 Hudson Street,
New York, New York 10014, USA
Penguin Group (Canada), 90 Eglinton Avenue East, Suite 700, Toronto,
Ontario M4P 2Y3, Canada (a division of Pearson Penguin Canada Inc.)
Penguin Books Ltd., 80 Strand, London WC2R 0RL, England
Penguin Ireland, 25 St. Stephen's Green, Dublin 2,
Ireland (a division of Penguin Books Ltd.)
Penguin Group (Australia), 250 Camberwell Road, Camberwell, Victoria 3124,
Australia (a division of Pearson Australia Group Pty. Ltd.)
Penguin Books India Pvt. Ltd., 11 Community Centre, Panchsheel Park,
New Delhi-110 017, India
Penguin Group (NZ), 67 Apollo Drive, Rosedale, North Shore 0632,
New Zealand (a division of Pearson New Zealand Ltd.)
Penguin Books (South Africa) (Pty.) Ltd., 24 Sturdee Avenue,
Rosebank, Johannesburg 2196, South Africa

Penguin Books Ltd., Registered Offices:
80 Strand, London WC2R 0RL, England

First published by Celebra,
a division of Penguin Group (USA) Inc.

First Printing, May 2008
10 9 8 7 6 5 4 3 2 1

Copyright © Mike Lowell and Rob Bradford, 2008
Foreword copyright © Josh Beckett, 2008
All rights reserved

CELEBRA and logo are trademarks of Penguin Group (USA) Inc.

LIBRARY OF CONGRESS CATALOGING-IN-PUBLICATION DATA:
Lowell, Mike.
    Deep drive: a long journey to finding the champion within/Mike Lowell with Rob Bradford;
with a foreword by Josh Beckett.
    p. cm.
    ISBN 978-0-451-22555-9
    1. Lowell, Mike.   2. Baseball players—United States—Biography.   I. Bradford, Rob, 1969– .
    II. Title.
GV865.L69L69 2008
796.357092—dc22   2008005284
[B]

Set in Iowan
Designed by Sabrina Bowers

Printed in the United States of America

Without limiting the rights under copyright reserved above, no part of this publication may be repro-
duced, stored in or introduced into a retrieval system, or transmitted, in any form, or by any means
(electronic, mechanical, photocopying, recording, or otherwise), without the prior written permission
of both the copyright owner and the above publisher of this book.

PUBLISHER'S NOTE
While the author has made every effort to provide accurate telephone numbers and Internet addresses
at the time of publication, neither the publisher nor the author assumes any responsibility for errors, or
for changes that occur after publication. Further, publisher does not have any control over and does not
assume any responsibility for author or third-party Web sites or their content.

The scanning, uploading, and distribution of this book via the Internet or via any other means without
the permission of the publisher is illegal and punishable by law. Please purchase only authorized electronic editions, and do not participate in or encourage electronic piracy of copyrighted materials. Your
support of the author's rights is appreciated.

To my kids, Alexis and Anthony,
may you always seek the positives
and learn from the negatives
in this wonderful ride called life.

—Your proud dad

Contents

Foreword

Josh Beckett

I remember it was toward the end of the 2007 regular season when I found myself sitting with David Ortiz back up in the clubhouse. Mike Lowell came on the television, getting ready for his turn at bat.

I turned to David and said, "Big Papi, you aren't going to be mad if I voted for Mikey for MVP, are you?"

"Hell, no," David said. "I would vote for him, too."

We won the World Series in '07, and Mike Lowell was one of the biggest reasons why.

But it wasn't just Mike Lowell the player whom we deemed so valuable. It was also Mike Lowell the person. To watch the success that Mike enjoyed during our run to the World Series title with the Red Sox was truly one of my most cherished highlights.

The guys in our clubhouse all knew Mike from being with the team for the previous two years, and had developed an enormous amount of respect for him during that stretch. But my admiration for Mike was born long before we both came to Boston. I had been with him in Florida the year after he survived cancer. We were together as part of a young bunch of Marlins who won the 2003 World Series. I saw the struggles that Mike went through during a 2005 season that wasn't up to his expectations.

And, of course, there was the day we became members of the Red Sox, coming over from Florida in the same trade.

Before the trade was made to the Sox, Mike and I knew we were most likely going to be a package deal. And that was fine with me. If I was going to take something from the Marlins with me to Boston, I couldn't think of anything, or anyone, better than Mike Lowell.

And then, two years after we talked on the phone with each other to confirm that we were indeed starting a new chapter of our lives, along comes the payoff for all of Mike's resiliency—the honor of being named the 2007 World Series MVP.

The minute Mike hit the home run in the seventh inning of game four of the World Series against Colorado, I knew he was going to be named the most valuable player. And that inclination was immediately followed with a sense of gratification and happiness.

I know when I won the award back in '03, there were plenty of guys in that clubhouse who had no idea who won the MVP of the series. A lot of times, you are simply too giddy to be worrying about such things. But I will guarantee you that knowing Mike had won this honor meant something special to the guys on our team. I know it did for me. Maybe better than anybody else in that dugout that night, I understood what Mike had gone through to get to that moment. And for me, that's what truly made the sight of him clutching the trophy, with that enormous smile, so special.

When I think of Mike Lowell, I think of all of our experiences, both the good times and the bad. But what truly jumps out upon the mention of his name is consistency. No matter what is happening—cancer, an off year, and all the ups and downs that come with being a major-league baseball player—Mike is consistent. I know that whatever bad times are presented to Mike, he is going to find the good in them and use that to overcome any adversity.

It has been an honor to know Mike, a man whose journey should be an inspiration to us all.

—JOSH BECKETT

DEEP DRIVE

Introduction

I still get choked up when I think about it.

Game on the line, one out, the other team brings in their hardest thrower, a runner on, and our team down by a run. The pitch comes and I hit one into the gap, past the fielders and into the expanse that is your typical fenceless Little League outfield. I round the bases for the game-winning home run, and for the first time in my young life, I find myself flush with the gratification befitting a hero.

But while the hit was nice—and believe me, when you're eight years old, it doesn't get much better—that's not what really gets me when remembering the moment.

A little later I was driving home with my dad, Carl, when he turned to me and said, "Doesn't it feel great to get that hit?" I told him it sure did, still reveling in my new role as third-grade baseball star.

He then added, "If you want to do that more often, you have to *want* to be the guy that's in that situation—because a lot of people say they want to be in that situation, but they don't want to be in that situation." Unbelievably, the glory of my home run had suddenly taken a backseat to these words. Even at that impatient age, listening to Dad was always the priority, and this was no exception.

"What's the worst that could happen?" Dad continued. "You make an out? Big deal. But if you *want* to be in that situation and you try your best, good things are going to happen."

I was eight years old! But you know what? I've followed his advice to this day because it really works. It worked in that moment I stepped up to the plate against one of the most feared flamethrowers in the Coral Gables Little League, and it worked on October 28, 2007.

Twenty-five years later I found myself driving away from another baseball field, once again soaking in the joy that came with playing a part in my team's victory. This time I was accompanied by my wife, Bertica, and our new best friend, the trophy signifying that I had been deemed by Major League Baseball as the most valuable player of the World Series.

I had hit .400 in the 2007 World Series, complete with a key seventh-inning home run in the game-four clincher, helping my Boston Red Sox beat the National League champion Colorado Rockies. I had heeded my dad's advice once again, desperately yearning to be put on the big stage so that I could revel in that feeling of accomplishment that was born on a Coral Gables Little League field.

Dad wasn't there in person this time; instead, he was

content to sit back at his home in South Florida with Mom, a rum and Coke, and his Sony television. A few hours earlier he had joined the millions upon millions of Red Sox fans in witnessing his son leap upon the pile of players on the Coors Field pitching mound, celebrating the right to be called the best of the baseball world.

"Unbelievable!" he shouted to me through the phone. "You crushed that ball to left. That was a great slide!"

Dad went on and on, finally pausing long enough for me to remind him, "Dad, I know. I'm the one who did it." Mom, usually a bit more introverted than her husband, was in the background screaming.

Unlike that trip from the field of my youth, on this ride home—or rather to an all-night party at the Palms Restaurant—there were no lessons to be learned. This was the payoff.

But after I got off the phone with my parents, the reflection began.

I started thinking about the path I took to find myself sitting next to this trophy and the wife I had first met at a luau at the tail end of my junior year of high school. I thought about my teammates and how they had come into my life. They didn't care that I was only there because the Red Sox were forced to take me in a trade with the Florida Marlins if they were going to get the blessed arm of Josh Beckett. All that mattered for all of us was that we were there, period.

There were the memories of my past as a 145-pound second baseman who switched schools just to live the dream of becoming a varsity high school baseball player, never mind entering into any fantasy of becoming a big leaguer.

I thought about the struggles my family overcame in escaping Cuba. I thought about how I had been a twentieth-round pick, and about the 2005 season that too many people to count had told me was the beginning of the end. And, of course, I thought about the cancer.

There was the day—February 19, 1999—I was told I had testicular cancer, the day I found out it was in remission, and then the day, four years later, I was informed the cancer had come back. That, in turn, was followed by the best day, the one when my family hugged, cried, and danced, while chanting the obscure medical term "fibrous dysplasia"—a much more palatable diagnosis—in the middle of my younger brother, Victor's, Gainesville apartment.

When Dad gave his advice to an eight-year-old still unwise to the ways of athletics, and the world in general, it was with a purpose. It was to the point, and with great resolve. My father had a knack for knowing just what to say and when to say it. It was his words that led me to the pantheon of baseball, his words to which I owe my World Series MVP trophy. But the effect of his words wasn't limited to my athletic achievement. These words also got me through life, as a five-hour ride to Gainesville in 2003 exemplified.

By the time July 2003 rolled around, I had found my "exclamation point" in the game—and in life. My battle to transform myself into something other than a singles-hitting third baseman, while fighting off the life-threatening disease that had been diagnosed four years earlier, had been won. I had become that prototypical power-hitting corner guy major-league baseball teams yearn to insert into their lineups. The Florida Marlins, my team since being traded from the New York Yankees in '99, were the ones reaping the dividends.

After the first half of the '03 season, I owned 28 home runs in 93 games, earning a ticket to my second All-Star Game. All was well, other than the fact that my hip had been tweaked in one of the games just prior to the break and was becoming increasingly sore with each passing day. I ended up claiming two hits while scoring a run during the game of stars in Milwaukee, but didn't hesitate in heading out of town the next day to go straight to the hospital for an MRI on the injured hip.

Then came the look. It was the same look I saw on the doctors' faces when they told me the bad news in '99. "Mike," said the doctor who was charged with analyzing the MRI, "I think you need to go to Dr. Kanell's office at Holy Cross Hospital." This wasn't the in-and-out kind of examination I was hoping for. Holy Cross was the same place I had been diagnosed with cancer four years earlier.

"Doc, I don't know if I should go," I said, desperately trying to hold on to my sense of humor. "I don't have a good history there."

At Holy Cross I found Dr. Daniel Kanell, the father of NFL quarterback Danny Kanell, and got him to look at the pictures of my lower half. A blow rivaling the diagnosis in '99 was about to be delivered.

"Mike, there's something on the MRI that came out, and it looks like cancer," he said.

This didn't add up. I immediately asked how this could be the case, since my doctors had told me all along that if my cancer was to return it would be in my lungs. Dr. Kanell said yes, that is usually the norm, but there was no getting around what he saw in front of him. To the untrained eye, it appeared like a big black ball, still intimidating even without the diagnosis. I exited the hospital a desperate man once again, this time with crutches for fear that a potential tumor might have begun to eat away at bone in my leg.

In my mind, this was even worse than '99. Back then I had been married for four months, but had no kids yet, so if something did happen it might be devastating for Bertica but life would go on for her. This time I had a daughter who was almost two years old. I would be leaving behind a child. The thought was too horrible to imagine. When I was diagnosed with cancer in '99, I never really asked, "Why me?" All I cared about was overcoming it. But this time, all I could think was, *How could this be happening to my daughter?*

An appointment was made to head up to Shands Medical Center in Gainesville, where both my sister, Ceci, and brother Victor were attending the University of Florida. For me, time was of the essence, and since there were no direct flights from Miami to the North Florida college town, I told my family we'd have to go by car. It would take five hours. I simply couldn't wait. So, along with Bertica and my parents, I started on the most anxiety-ridden road trip of my life.

This is where Dad stepped up once again.

Giving advice was easy for my father, but this time he was faced with the five-hour challenge of doing everything but. I appreciated the miles and miles of silence—it gave me time to find whatever peace of mind I could muster. But when the quiet became too much for all of us to bear, Dad came in with talk of the Marlins and the All-Star Game I had just returned from. The names of Josh Beckett, Brad Penny, Miguel Cabrera, and Dontrelle Willis lightened the heavy mood in the car as we made our way to Gainesville. As always, this time with Dad somehow gave me a clearer view on life, even though we both knew things could be getting awfully cloudy in the very near future.

What I didn't realize at the time was that the situation had pushed my father to a place he never thought he would find himself. For the first and only time in his life, Dad was angry at God. This man, who had lived his life as a devout Catholic, was taken over by thoughts that flew in the face of everything he believed. He was asking, "Why?"

We got into Gainesville at about two in the morning and booked two rooms at the only hotel that was still open, the Days Inn. One-star, five-star—the surroundings didn't matter that night. I wasn't going to sleep, but I was going to worry. Thankfully Bertica was there by my side all night, telling me that everything was going to be fine, that I had overcome before and I would overcome again.

Other than Bertica and my parents, no one knew what was going on. I was missing that first game back from the All-Star break, but the explanation was that I was simply having some tests done on my sore hip. I had even registered into the medical center under an alias. The Gainesville doctor, Mark Scarborough, also went so far as to have us meet him at a nearby food court before I underwent the tests, preventing any possibility of someone connecting the dots and figuring out this might be more than a strained hip. The last thing I wanted was for word to get out.

Once we were in the lab room, which was pretty empty over the weekend, Dr. Scarborough laid out the scenario that he believed could be unfolding. He explained that while it might be cancer, there is also a condition that sometimes appears on MRIs that looks like humungous freckles and is often mistaken for the worst. The condition was called fibrous dysplasia.

Fibrous dysplasia accounts for about 7 percent of all benign bone tumors, and is a chronic condition that develops before birth, as a result of the abnormal growth of a particular bone within the womb. Whatever it is, it sounded a whole lot better than bone cancer.

Dr. Scarborough continued: "Now, I'm not saying you have this, but I am saying this is a possibility, because for your type of cancer to end up in a bone the way it is on this MRI is highly unlikely."

The tests began, but since the college was closed at the time, the Saturday examination was somewhat of a makeshift operation. Dr. Scarborough had taken it upon himself to ensure privacy, conducting all of the tests himself, even such a routine task as drawing blood. This wasn't the norm for someone of his stature, as was evidenced by his forgoing of a rubber band to find the needle's landing spot. No, he was definitely a pro. But he was intent on doing this in a discreet way. And for that, I was glad.

The blood was taken, with the tumor markers (substances produced by the body in response to cancer growth) identified. Unfortunately, I had come to know the drill. After that, all we could do was wait. So we did, heading over to my brother's apartment across town in anticipation of a phone call.

This—not draft day, not the day of the initial cancer diagnosis, not anything I had ever encountered—was the longest wait of my life. Then the call came.

"Mike," the doctor said, "I have two colleagues here, and they are both very well respected in the field. I had each of them look, independently, at the reports and my results. In each case, I gave you a different name as an alias. I then asked them, 'What is your analysis of this MRI, blood work, CT scan, et cetera, et cetera?'"

Okay, and . . .

"All three of us say it's fibrous dysplasia."

Holy shit!

The celebration was on. There we were, in the middle of my brother's apartment, jumping up and down like we would at home plate after a walk-off home run.

"Fibrous dysplasia! Fibrous dysplasia!"

We couldn't stop saying the words. My parents, covered in tears, were yelling them out. My sister and brother joined in. And Bertica and I couldn't stop screaming.

"Fibrous dysplasia! Fibrous dysplasia."

No sweeter expression had ever been uttered. This cancer was nothing more than a big-ass freckle. I can say with great certainty that the Ballyhoo Grill, the most convenient eating establishment we could find near the hotel, has never had a party with more smiles than the one the Lowell family brought in their doors later that night.

Less than a week later, I was back on the baseball field. I had endured once again. There would be more obstacles in the not-so-distant future, and more joy. But no matter what happened, it was going to be hard to top hearing those two words: "fibrous dysplasia."

As we drove home from Gainesville, both my father and I knew in the back of our minds that life would be sending more curveballs our way sometime soon. Our family had gotten used to dealing with a steady stream of benders. These were, after all, what made my story my story, and my life my life. For now I was intent on enjoying the happiness of the present.

CHAPTER ONE
Beginnings

Journal entry, February 11, 2007

I cannot believe so much time has gone by. First, eight games left in the season, and now eight days left before spring training. Let's start with the off-season being great. Too short. Seems they get shorter each year. Sign of a true veteran. Feel good and healthy going into the year. Trained hard, hit well, am in shape. Really want to get with [Red Sox mental performance coach] Donny Kalkstein early to get my thoughts in the right place.

Was not happy about the possible trade to Colorado. Lose-lose situation. God, I love to win and winning there is almost impossible. No pitching.

Trained well, not as regimented but love doing the running program with Victor. What a brother. We are very similar. Went back to the same running program as in 2003. Hopefully will have a similar year.

I really connected with my son, Anthony, this off-season. I love riding the bike and pitching to him. Can't wait to get him to Fenway. What kid can play with his dad at Fenway Park!! He is talking a lot more, but can be feisty. Can't say I mind it. Better than being a pushover.

My daughter, Alexis, is fabulous. Loves numbers, and Chutes and Ladders. Always asking me or Bertica to play. Great mix, likes numbers and board games, like Dad, but enjoys her dolls like Mom did. She is so cute with a great independent personality.

I pledged for New Year's one entry per month, so I guess I am one month behind. Overall, life is still good! Me.

B y the time I found myself at the end of Edison Avenue in Fort Myers, pulling into the Red Sox minor-league training facility for another spring training, life was good. Different, but good.

There was a peace of mind surrounding me that had been missing for some time. It was a serenity that had only recently taken root. I had started to realize how happy I was playing in Boston, and I shuddered at the prospect of having to switch teams once again. The Red Sox were contemplating shipping me in a package of players to Colorado in exchange for the Rockies' first baseman, Todd Helton. No, thanks. Living the life of a Red Sox was my cool side of the pillow, and I was far from ready to have to establish a new comfort zone.

I liked that fans were lined up along the hot Florida sidewalk to get a glimpse of their team playing catch on the first day of workouts. And I relished sitting in the middle of a familiar clubhouse talking baseball with my teammates, whom I had gotten to know over the '06 season.

Familiarity in baseball is a valued commodity, and I felt it very strongly as I entered into my second spring training with the Red Sox.

In a strange way I was also relieved to see the media's focus shift from my locker to wherever the new batch of stories resided—our new $103 million Japanese starting pitcher, Daisuke Matsuzaka, for example, or the team's other big off-season investment, the soft-spoken outfielder J. D. Drew.

Throughout my roller-coaster ride I have learned that you have to look for positives, because there will always be negatives. In '07 the positives were now waiting around every corner. But a year before, that wasn't exactly the case.

Sure, some things were the same for me at spring training in '06 and '07. Seeing David Ortiz's smile when I arrived. Hearing Curt Schilling boast of his fantasy football acumen. The thousands of spectators watching us limber up. This is what I loved about the Red Sox. When I was with the Marlins, we had to give away T-shirts (and our firstborn) to play in front of a full house for a spring-training game. I liked it when there was fireworks night in the minor leagues and you got to play in front of a full house. And here, with the Red Sox, I was being cheered just for jogging around the field.

But a year before, I wasn't so sure how it was going to turn out. When it came to preparing for a season, I had never experienced anything like the days leading up to my first year in Boston.

Batting average: .236. Home runs: 8.

This was the reality of my '05 season. And these grim numbers were all the more inexplicable given that I was coming off perhaps the best year of my career in '04, during which I finished hitting .293 with 27 homers. By the end of my nightmare final campaign with the Marlins, I was finding it pretty hard to come up with any kind of positive spin on the situation.

All that time all I wanted was to put '05 behind me—and I saw the chance to get a fresh start in Boston. I had been thrown what I viewed as a pretty appetizing opportunity, and, really, that's all I could have asked for. That's all I have ever asked for.

But no matter which team I would wind up playing for in '06, what I wanted, first and foremost, was to prove people wrong. Admittedly, some of my drive came from a selfish place within. These critics—none of them were ever in the cage with me when I was working through my struggles in '05; none of them was in the weight room with me. They just wanted to look at the numbers and make judgments about my swing and what type of athlete I am.

"His bat speed is no longer there." I heard that one a lot from these anonymous scouts. *Are you kidding me? When did they whip out the bat-speed monitor?* That was how I thought.

But even before the end of the '05 season, or the trade to the Red Sox, I was intent on shifting my focus for the future. From the final month of my misery, all the way until I made that February trip across Florida to Boston's spring-training home, I was going to live by the same premise I had in the minor leagues. When you're a twentieth-round pick, you have no choice but to impress in spring training. The plan was to come in game-ready, and that would, in turn, start pushing aside any questions, doubts, or mythical bat-speed monitors. But for all that to happen I needed to track down an old friend: Gary Denbo.

Denbo was one of my minor-league hitting coaches in the Yankee organization, and if there was anybody who understood how I went from point A to point Z, it was Gary. The problem was, as I found out in early September of '05, he was now coaching in Japan. So a hands-on approach wouldn't be an immediate option. But I e-mailed him anyway and he got right back to me, instructing me on how we could talk through his computer and my phone. Bingo.

"What's the problem?" he asked.

"I think I've lost the ability to stay direct to the ball," I responded. Not staying "direct to the ball" suggested I was swinging up, down, sideways, and everywhere else that wasn't putting my swing on the optimum plane needed to place the maximum amount of wood on the largest possible area of the baseball. That immediately spawned a whole new checklist of concerns from Gary's standpoint.

"Are you hurt?" he said. Negative.

"What do you feel?" Gary continued. I told him that every time I felt like I was getting my pitch, I was fouling it off. "Well, *where* are you fouling it off?" he responded. I answered that I would usually hook it foul, oftentimes getting underneath it. Normally, attempting to find swing solutions through a computer line stretching from Japan to Florida would not be the ideal scenario, but even though Gary hadn't diagnosed the problem yet, I already had the feeling that this connection was paving the way for some answers.

"Okay," said Gary, "it's a bit difficult for me because I haven't seen you in four years. But I want you to just remember the fundamentals. The thing that has always worked for you is putting the hitting tee really inside and exaggerating that you have to hit that ball inside, up the middle. It might not be what you want to do in games, but it is the path you want your mind to remember." That, alone, made me feel a bit of optimism, which had been a foreign concept for months. (It had gotten a slight bit better in the last ten games of the '05 season, when I had managed a .306 batting average, getting at least a single in all but one of the games.) The conversation with Gary had been short, but when it came to his overseas wisdom, quality, not quantity, was all that mattered.

In particular, Gary's mentioning the hitting tee struck a chord with me. Some guys have no use for an inanimate piece of rubber tubing when it comes to fine-tuning their swing, but for me it has been the foundation of all my fix-it projects. I started using it in high school, but more because our team was into drill work and that tee was always available. In college, at Florida International, I liked to go to the cage before practice, but I had nobody to throw to me so the tee was my only option. It wasn't fancy, but, for me, it was effective. I liked the fact you could go at your own pace. If you wanted to take ten swings in thirty seconds you could do that, or if you would rather take ten swings in ten minutes, that could be your regimen. The tee allowed you to manipulate how you wanted to hit the ball, where you wanted to hit the ball, and when you wanted to hit the ball.

The bottom line is that, tee or no tee, a hitting coach can tell you what he sees, but he can never tell how you feel. You're the only one who can answer that.

By the time the baseball playoffs had come and gone, Gary's contract had expired in Japan, and he was back in Tampa, just a few hours away, so I didn't have to rely on the miracle of modern technology to untangle my career. We decided that I was going to hop on a plane with nothing but a video camera and some bats, but only after shipping him footage of both my mind-numbing '05 season and the good times that were the two previous campaigns. It was thanks to those tapes that Gary was able to identify a big part of my problem before I even packed my bags for the cross-state business trip.

Gary e-mailed me after watching the good, bad, and ugly that came with three seasons of swings: "It seems like the only balls you put in play hard are balls that were on the outer third of the plate, and you pulled those to left field. You're coming around on the ball every time." You know how sometimes people give you advice and you want it to fit your problem so badly that you start implementing a mental sledgehammer to make it fit? Well, that wasn't the case here. I knew right away that Gary had hit on something important.

I immediately flashed back to a conversation I had had with one of my teammates, Jeff Conine, three months earlier.

I had been talking to Conine about how over the last four-plus months none of the pitches that came to me from the middle of the plate and in—usually the greatest gift a pitcher could offer my thirty-two-ounce Louisville Slugger—had resulted in a hard hit. And now Gary was telling me why. I wasn't giving myself a chance to hit the ball hard. I was, as he explained, "coming around the ball" too early and too often. Problem diagnosed, but hardly solved. That's why I was leaving my family for a few days with hardly anything more than a bagful of wood and some video equipment.

Some might have viewed this as a random, even desperate, leap of faith. And maybe it was. But I wasn't going to sit still while the slings and arrows flew by, attempting to drive me into baseball's abyss at the age of thirty-one.

My first session with Gary in Tampa was mercifully elementary. It was nothing more than simple work off the hitting tee, with Gary and the video camera behind me. "Hit the ball up the middle," he would say, "and remember how your muscles felt when you did that." And every time I did it right, Gary's positive reinforcement would come in the form of a simple wave in front of the camera's lens. He was identifying the swings he wanted me to see and emulate time and time again. I focused on making Gary's hand go up as many times as I could.

It wasn't until my third day that pitches were actually thrown. My hands had become a bit sore from so much hitting, but the pain was no match for the excitement I felt. My back-spin was back—that is to say, when I was hitting the ball, the bat was finding the baseball with a directness that I thought had gone on permanent hiatus. Despite what the bat-speed monitors of those anonymous scouts said, getting to the ball on time was never really an issue. Guys were throwing 97 miles per hour, and I was not only right on them but often-times coming around too early.

By the time I packed up my bags and camera, ready to head home, the thought of spring training suddenly didn't in-duce that sit-on-a-cactus kind of trepidation I had been fight-ing since the end of the '05 season. My enthusiasm had returned, along with a good portion of my swing. And when I went back to the hitting cages in mid-December, nearly a month earlier than my usual routine, I instantly knew which swings were the keepers. And just in case they didn't leave a lasting impression, I had taken the time to institute Gary's method of waving to the camera. Strangely enough, the blurry image of a hand on my television became the ultimate security blanket as I headed into the introduction with my new team.

By the time I cruised down Route 41 and onto the road to Fort Myers, it had been three months since I last worked with Gary. He had been hired by the Yankees and, after my trade to Boston, we both decided that a Yankees coach instructing a member of the Red Sox wouldn't have been greeted with a bouquet of flowers from New York owner George Steinbren-ner. I was on my own with just my revamped swing and newly found confidence, and that was fine with me. But as I was about to discover, somebody else thought they had the answers, too.

Now, it's perfectly normal for coaches, when they meet you for the first time, to try to strike a rapport. And that's exactly what the Red Sox hitting coach Ron "Papa Jack" Jackson tried to do upon our introduction. "You know," said Papa Jack, "I've been looking at your film, and there are a couple of things I see." Wait a second. I'm thinking about having worked on this stuff my whole off-season, and now we're going to go in another direction?

But Papa Jack was, and is, enthusiastic. He started talking about my stride foot, and this and that. I got the feeling that he was looking for the perfect swing, and from where I was coming from, that kind of expectation wasn't an option, or even a necessity. But I was the new kid, and Papa Jack, who was clearly well-intentioned, just wanted to help me figure out what had ailed me the year before. But by the fifth day of spring training, he had me trying so many new things that it was starting to feel like '05 all over again. I'd make an adjustment here, an adjustment there, and before you know it, I've made twenty-five adjustments and it's June. That's what happened to me before, when I was looking for a quick fix instead of simply grinding it out myself. I needed to trust myself. In my quest for positives after my depressing '05 season, this was a lesson I wasn't about to let go of.

Again, when it comes to finding the best hitting coach, looking in the mirror is always the best place to start. Only you know how you feel each day, if your body is tired, and if you feel a little quick or a little slow. And ultimately that's what I had to tell Papa Jack: "I can't try a new thing every day. I can't do it. Just because batting practice doesn't work out for a couple of rounds, I've still got to believe in the work that I have done and that I did in the off-season. Let's let the game get started, go from there, and talk as it progresses." I enjoyed working with Papa Jack because he is always willing to try to get it done. But I simply didn't want to make all those adjustments. I had to try to solve the problem myself instead of waiting for the problem to be solved for me. New team or not, that was me. That's always been my way.

I truly came to understand how important it is to rely on yourself as the ultimate hitting instructor after talking to the former batting champ Tony Gwynn. My old teammate, Mark Kotsay, knew I would have loved to talk shop with Gwynn concerning hitting, so he set it up. "Just come over when Tony is near me, I will ask him a question about hitting and he will go off," Kotsay said. So when the opportunity arose, I sidled up next to Mark with Tony right there, Mark mentioned something about hitting, and Gwynn started waxing poetic.

Tony went on to talk about how he really focuses on taking the knob of the bat to the ball. That was the most important thing to concentrate on in his mind. If it was good enough for one of the greatest hitters of all time, it was going to be good enough for me. The very next batting-practice session I was all excited about breaking out my new knowledge. Twenty pitches proceeded to come in, each of which I took the knob to the ball. Or at least that's what I thought I was doing. Every single one of those pitches was fouled straight up in the air. There wasn't a solid hit among the session. I couldn't comprehend how this could be. How could Tony Gwynn steer me astray?

The lesson was that what he was describing most likely was something I might describe in a different way, such as hitting through the ball. What worked for him didn't work for me, and that was fine. He was his best hitting coach, and I was mine. It was something I was forced to remind myself of during that first spring with the Sox.

Still, my turnaround was creeping along slower than anticipated. And Boston is not the kind of place where you want to get off to a slow start, as I would soon find out.

One of my former Florida teammates, Kevin Millar, who played with the Red Sox before I came aboard, had bombarded me with tales about how great it was to live the life of a professional Boston baseball player. His all-encompassing endorsement stretched from the greatness of Terry Francona, to the guys in the clubhouse, and even to a Web site called Boston Dirt Dogs.

Millar told me I would be blown away by how this Internet site was a constant stream of information regarding the Red Sox and dwarfed anything we might have come across as members of the Marlins. He made it seem like cyberspace nirvana. It sounded like just the dose of fun I needed. But then I went 1 for my first 7 in spring training and the flip side of the fans' passion slapped me across the face.

"Lowell's done!"

"Move Youk to third!"

The brutal headlines on the Web site and elsewhere kept coming with each spring-training groundout. Millar was full of crap. This wasn't cool. I thought people paying attention to all the minute details of a baseball game was going to be fun, and, as I've come to learn, most of the time it is. But you had just better not go 1 for 7 to start spring training.

I called Bertica and said, "If anyone tells you about anything that's in the Boston papers, don't tell me about it because I don't want to get caught up in the negativity." If things weren't going to work out in this, one of the most important spring trainings of my career, then let it be because I couldn't hit a ball through the infield or over the fence, not because of these outside negative forces. My credo about looking for the positives and not the negatives was getting tougher and tougher to sustain, but it managed to keep me going through my introductory month with the Red Sox.

Walking the media tightrope was nothing new to me. When you go through what I did in '05, everybody wants an answer, and it is the journalists' jobs to find it. But I never seemed to give them the kind of answer they desired. There was no great white whale (such as steroids) in my story. Also, I tended to follow a helpful piece of advice passed along by the former major leaguer Andre Dawson. When talking about his approach toward the media, Dawson said, "I kept giving them the same boring answer, and then they didn't ask me the same stupid questions."

Another big part of the equation was patience, something

I learned a thing or two about during my short time within the Yankees' major-league clubhouse. My locker was right next to Scott Brosius's, I was two spots from Derek Jeter, and other veteran guys, Tino Martinez and Paul O'Neill, weren't too far away. The personalities were all different—Tino being a steady type of guy, Paul wanting to throw a bat every single time he made an out, and Derek playing the cool part of the young fan favorite. But all of them understood what the media was about and none of them lost their temper when questions were thrown their way. When big-market teams are involved, provocative stories are inevitably going to be written—just to spark things up. All of these guys knew this, but they still never lost their cool and always remained positive. That, I determined, was the way to do it.

There is, however, always a boiling point, no matter how even-keeled your approach might be. This I discovered in 2005.

As I was hitting rock bottom performance-wise, there was a story in the paper about how my skills had disappeared. On the front page of the sports section, it was the centerpiece article, and then on the inside, it took up an entire page. It was definitely the most prominent sports piece that day. It went on and on, but all of the material came from an anonymous source here, a scout there, an unnamed coach. Everything was from these anonymous people talking about my slow bat, lack of power, even the insinuation that I was using performance-enhancing drugs. That's when I felt obligated, for the first time in my career, to confront a writer.

"I understand you can write anything you want, and everyone knows that I'm not having a good year, but what I don't understand about this article is that you didn't ask me one question," I said to him. "There's not one of my quotes in here. I see six anonymous sources, so you took the time to try and find six people that apparently you want to protect, or you just made up. Either way, it doesn't matter to me. I don't have a problem with the substance of what you wrote, but how do you make a cover story and not ask me one question? You're telling me how things are, but why don't you go to the horse's mouth? I could have made your story better, but you're going to drop this on me without even a heads-up that this is coming out? You're just going to lay a hammer on me?"

He went on to say that it was out of respect for me. He was waiting to talk to me because he believed I would be coming out of my funk. That was ridiculous. I stood there taking questions from reporters every single game, and, more often than not, it was to talk about the negatives. I made myself more than available for him to come up and ask me my side of the story, yet he chose to hide. In another first, I told the writer he wouldn't be getting any more quotes from me.

A year later we were on a road trip and he showed up. "Are we cool?" he asked. "What do you mean, are we cool? Yeah, we're cool," I told him. "I'm not going to punch you or anything." He then asked if he could get a couple of words from me. The answer probably wasn't what he, or his paper, wanted to hear: "Well, I'm sorry you wasted your money on your plane ticket." And that was it. He would pop up again when we

played the Marlins, and I told him that he was more than welcome to stand in and listen to all the other questions, but if he
opened his mouth, I wouldn't be talking to anyone.

Maybe over time he realized he had made a bit of a mistake. I would at least like to think so. I know it was an awakening for me. That '05 season was a struggle, and while I didn't
need any more negativity, I still tried to treat people as fairly
and decently as I could, even in the worst of times. But that
guy still threw me under the bus.

I also realized after going through that first month with
the Red Sox that shutting out the world in times of need isn't
the smartest approach. So I did let people in, and, as it turned
out, those were the influences that pushed me along the right
path and ultimately led me to standing on Coors Field as the
MVP of the 2007 World Series.

One of the more important sounding boards was the Red
Sox mental performance coach, Don Kalkstein, who was also
in his first year with the team. While his title is a bit
convoluted—he is basically a sports psychologist—the results
he produces are anything but. It was a good fit in the sense
that I'm a guy who believes in coaching the mental aspect of
the game, from heeding the advice of my father about yearning to be placed upon the biggest stages to convincing myself
that being a Red Sox was going to be a good thing, for both me
and the team.

Think of it this way: Most outstanding people in the
business world go to these seminars because there is always
somebody out there who might know something they don't,

something that could help them. It's not a weakness—it's what you do so you can get better, and, man, did I want to get better.

Donny is a very approachable guy, not at all overbearing. If you want to talk to him, he will talk, and usually you will learn. I did. He was a crucial part of the metamorphosis I went through during '06 spring training.

"When you were in Little League, were you a good player?" he asked.

"Absolutely," I said.

"Were you an All-Star player?" he continued.

"Yeah, I was."

"Did you ever worry about your hands or your feet at the plate?"

"No."

"Then how did you know you were good?"

I told him I knew because I got a lot of hits.

"Well," Donny said, "did you play Wiffle ball growing up?" This was a no-brainer. I had played the backyard game virtually every day for five years.

The questions kept coming. "Did you ever worry about staying inside the ball in Wiffle ball?" No. "Well, were you a good hitter in Wiffle ball?" Yes. "Then why don't you pretend you're playing Wiffle ball?" he suggested. "Mike, I know how to have the mind-set. This is what I studied. But I don't have the talent to hit. Everyone would love to hit and you have the talent to hit. You've had it for six years. I don't care about last year. I want you to go out there and not worry about anything and just hit the ball. You're cluttering your mind with so much stuff."

The next time I went to the plate, I was playing Wiffle ball. The usual thoughts of looking for a fastball near the middle of the plate or even farther inside, or sitting back on an off-speed offering, were gone. If the ball looked good, I was going to swing, and whatever happened, happened.

What happened was I got a hit, and another, and another. And not only that, but those hits were often hard, the kind of swings that would have elicited a healthy amount of video-taped Gary Denbo hand waving. A childhood of successfully hitting a perforated plastic ball with a rail-thin yellow bat was finally paying dividends.

Another voice, besides Donny, who really made an impression throughout that first March with the Red Sox was that of my new manager, Terry "Tito" Francona. Sometime right around the middle of the month, when the hits were just starting to drop but home runs remained hard to find, he said, "Mike, you're here for two years. I've seen you play. You're going to play, so just have fun and relax." It might not have seemed like much, but coming from the man who would be writing my name in the lineup, it was reassuring.

I started to really appreciate Tito. The best thing about him, as I have learned, is that he lets guys be themselves. He tells us out of the chute in spring training that there aren't many rules, but that we should use our common sense. He understands that wearing suits on flights doesn't necessarily make you win or lose ball games. For him, it's important that players feel comfortable to be themselves, as long as they can show him that they understand how to be prepared. If you take advantage of the latitude, you will get clamped down on. But usually what happens is that the young guys see how the veterans go about their routine and follow suit. It's a good environment, and, to me, that all stems from Tito.

But what really stands out when I think about Tito is how he protects that atmosphere. There are times when he is almost called upon to talk badly about his own players in the media, and he never does it, never. Don't get me wrong. There are some tense closed-door meetings with certain guys, and the ups and downs of a 162-game regular season will always spawn some prickliness. None of it, however, will be fueled by a Terry Francona comment in the newspaper. There are managers who use the media to get under their players' skin, trying to send a message. For me, that isn't the right way. Sometimes it may work, but not when you're trying to build trust and support among a locker room full of characters from all corners of the globe. Evidently, Tito agrees.

Bottom line, he just wants you to win, man. He really wants to win. And what makes it even better is that he thinks he's a good cribbage player, too, which is fantastic because I love taking his money.

From our first introduction I hoped that Tito knew he could rely on me. But I also understood it would be somewhat of a blind faith. Francona knew I had a solid reputation. But he had no idea what made up the real me, what I call my foundation, and how it had been built on the sacrifices of others.

Even in the chaos of turning my career around, I never forgot, and never will.

Those in Boston who didn't comprehend the nature of my family's story were introduced to a reality I knew all too well thanks to a front-page article in the *Boston Herald* midway through my first season with the Red Sox. The Cuban dictator Fidel Castro was reportedly very ill, prompting some reporters who knew my relatives' struggles under his regime to ask my thoughts on the subject. I understood that in our corner of the world, I was the connection to the story.

The next day a portion of my comment, along with cutout photos of myself and Castro, took up most of the front page. "I Hope He Dies" were the words splashed across the top. That morning an old schoolmate of mine who lived in Boston text-messaged me, urging me to check out the *Herald*. I thought it must be related to something involving the previous night's game, so I waited until I got to the park before taking a look. "Oh . . . my . . . goodness!" People who saw my reaction assumed I thought my comment had been blown out of proportion, but the truth was that it wasn't. The truth was that it was more real than most could comprehend.

I had also explained to the reporters where my anger came from. You have to understand, this was a man who had killed a family member of mine, imprisoned numerous other family members, violated human rights left and right, and forced people to become so desperate to escape his reign that they would go into an ocean knowing only one of four would make it, while the other three would most likely be eaten by sharks. There are tens of thousands of brothers, sisters, sons, daughters, husbands, and wives who have suffered atrocities at the hands of this man. So that's where my hatred came from. It might not have been the right thing to say, or something easily understood, but it was from the heart.

If I had said, that same day, "I hope Osama bin Laden dies," everybody would have nodded their heads in approval because his evil is in the here and now. But for me, Castro's evil is always present. If you get to know my story, get to know my family, and what they have had to endure, you will understand why I have this utter hatred. You will start to understand what I see as my foundation.

And this foundation begins with the name I was born with: Michael Averett Vogt-Lowell. The "Vogt" has since been legally removed, but its symbolism will never be cast aside. The surname was that of my great-grandfather, Carl Vogt, the man who set our family's triumph in motion.

It was the early part of the twentieth century and Carl Vogt set off by ship from his native Germany—where times were tough economically—to Culiacán, Mexico, where he hoped to find his fortune. But after spending a short time in Mexico, Vogt reunited with his wife's sisters, who had found their way to Chicago. Believe it or not, it was this journey to the Windy City that led to my family's roots in Cuba. Vogt had begun to work in a meatpacking plant in Chicago, when he and a few of his Spanish-speaking coworkers were summoned to help start an offshoot of the facility in Cuba, where lots of people cooked with the pig grease the Chicago-based company was simply throwing away.

By the time the 1930s hit, not only had my great-grandfather become a Cuban resident, but his son, my grandfather, had been given an extra name. Carl Vogt-Lowell had taken on his mother's maiden name, Lowell, as was customary in the island nation. My great-grandfather felt much more Cuban than German by this point. And my grandfather, who was born in Chicago, an American citizen, had little connection with his German roots. Nevertheless, both men were about to be subjected to their first taste of Cuban oppression, thanks to the anti-German sentiment that was surrounding United States' interests.

With the island's venom pointed directly at anybody with a German connection, my grandfather and his father were identified as problems in the eyes of the Cuban government solely because of the German-influenced "Vogt" in their names. The result was life-altering: Both men were placed in an anti-German internment camp for more than two years at a place called Isla de Pinos. For no reason other than a German last name, a father and son were taken from their home and family. It was the first of many scars that Cuba left on our family.

My grandfather, in particular, had a difficult time understanding his family's plight. He wanted to enter the military and fight the Germans, not embrace their ways. At the same time, he was not going to allow his father to enter the camp alone, so he paid the price along with the original Carl Vogt. It would leave a lasting effect on my grandfather, one that he would take out on his father's former homeland, Germany, almost immediately after being released from Isla de Pinos.

My grandfather, the man who spoke perfect English, perfect Spanish, and German from his father's influence, ultimately dropped the "Vogt" and entered the United States military as a paratrooper for the final few years of World War II. Carl Lowell was going to prove, once and for all, that he was truly an American. The anxiety of jumping out of an airplane was nothing compared to the fear he had lived through in the camp. And while his dad might not have been at his side ten thousand feet in the air, over enemy lines, he never left my grandfather's thoughts.

After the war my grandfather found himself working for a company in California, where another Carl Vogt-Lowell was born, my own father. When my dad was two years old, he went with his father back to Cuba, where the family would stay until he turned eleven. By this time, of course, there was no more internment camp, no more rage against people of German descent, but an entirely new type of pain had been introduced to the people of Cuba. Fidel Castro's reign had taken root.

As 1960 rolled in, my father had already established himself as one of the better eleven-year-old baseball players in his part of Cuba. But despite his fledgling baseball career, his parents had come to grips with the fact that the life that lay ahead of them under the new system was not worth playing it safe for. That's why, when an opportunity to exit the island presented itself, my grandfather, grandmother, and their four children didn't hesitate to move on from what had become their heritage.

My grandfather was now presented with the chance to escape to Puerto Rico, from where an acquaintance had gotten word to him that there was a job available selling bathroom tiles. The family could leave, but the deal was that each person was allowed no more than one suitcase for the entirety of their possessions, along with $125 for each adult, and $5 per child. They would get to San Juan, although this new life meant sharing a three-bedroom house with a single bathroom . . . for fifteen people.

As bad as it was, in their eyes it was still a better situation than where they had come from.

Evidence of the pain inflicted by Castro's regime isn't hard to find in our family, and not just on my side. My wife is also Cuban and her father, Jose Lopez, was jailed as a political prisoner by the government for fifteen years.

The story of how he met my future mother-in-law is remarkable. Along with her sister and mother, she was placed on a list to request departure from the island. Once you were placed on that list, you were considered a traitor, and as a result you were forced to pay your dues in the form of work, such as picking tomatoes, corn, etc. While going to visit a family member, she came across a political prisoner who had guards surrounding him at a bus stop. That man turned out to be her future husband, Jose Lopez.

Jose, as part of a rehabilitation program after five months

in group confinement for refusing to be indoctrinated, was given the opportunity to visit a dying uncle. The two spoke at the bus stop and formed an instant bond. They exchanged information and began a courtship of letters and the occasional jail visit for the next three years.

It was enough of a bond that when the departure request was granted, she chose the promise of love rather than freedom for the time being. While her mother and sister accepted the invitation to the United States, she spent years writing to Jose in Cuba.

Finally, as the relationship grew stronger, Jose's love knew a priest who joined her in going to the prison to marry the pair. Now, being a married prisoner, he was given more latitude during visitation hours. The marriage was forced to develop with Lopez still calling jail his home. It was during one of those visits that my wife was conceived, with Bertica's birth coming in 1974. Castro had never been able to stop this family, and my wife offered the ultimate example.

Three years after the birth of his daughter, Jose caught a break. One of the prisoners he had developed a close friendship with was extradited to Venezuela, where he was subsequently allowed to make a list of people he could mandate be released from the Cuban prisons. He could name a hundred people, and the first one on that list was my father-in-law. As Jose describes it, there was a bond between many of the prisoners, because not only were they in the same hellish situation, but they were there for the same reason—their beliefs. Nothing more. Fifteen years in jail because you stick to your beliefs.

Upon his release, Jose moved his new family to Venezuela as well, before settling three years later in their ultimate landing spot, Miami.

Which is where I ended up meeting Bertica years later. I still think about all of the different obstacles overcome by so many of our family members. The prisons, the tortures, the idea that you could be so miserable that leaving an entire life behind is the only option. I think of my mother having to sew her family's valuables into her dress as a little girl to circumvent the rule limiting a human being's life to one suitcase. This is what I call my foundation. This is what the managers, teammates, and organizations often don't consider, but they should. This is the making of me.

In the world of baseball, chances to take the easy road are littered throughout every 162-game season. But my family has supplied me with some powerful reminders of why it's important to stay true to yourself and to the journey you set out to begin with.

I took this attitude with me going into spring training in '07. At that time, everyone was focused on the batch of newcomers, but I wasn't about to make any quick judgments. Sure, there were first impressions, which were hard to ignore when it came to the kind of talent we were watching in Daisuke Matsuzaka, J. D. Drew, and Julio Lugo. But no fast-and-firm judgments.

It was hard to get an accurate gauge on guys like Daisuke and Julio since neither was among the teammates I had joined in bouncing from field to field in the early days of spring. But J.D. was another matter because he was in my hitting group. Again, there were no judgments, but there were impressions, and he left a pretty good one. His presentation was unique, in my eyes—it almost seems like he's bored when he hits because his whole approach is so calm. But then, just as you're lulled to sleep by the stillness of his stance, boom! He absolutely explodes. He had "the tools"—the physical measuring sticks by which players are usually identified at an early stage—but he also had the ability to hit the ball wherever the pitch dictated it should be hit.

As I saw more of J.D., and I saw the speed of Lugo—and various other pieces we didn't have a year before—I began to believe that we might really have something. No spring training is without trepidation, but this time it was nice to be anxious about the big picture rather than about whether I was going to make the grade on the bat-speed monitor.

One uneasy feeling I was starting to get revolved around Jonathan Papelbon. After he had served as one of the game's most dominant relief pitchers the year before, he was put into the starting rotation. The organization thought the regularity of this scenario would be the best thing for his right shoulder, where he had experienced a subluxation in the final month of '06. But during the times I talked to Pap, I could sense that he really enjoyed the lifestyle of the closer, and leaving his adrenaline on the sidelines in the four days between starts might not be his thing.

Pap is awesome. He is so intense and focused on the field.

He is the perfect guy to put the punctuation on baseball games. And the ideal player when it comes to building a team that is united and works together. He simply can't imagine any kind of language or cultural barrier coming into play in the clubhouse. And his work ethic! Pap reminds me of the guy in the movie *This Is Spinal Tap* who put all of the dials on the amplifier to eleven instead of the usual ten for the simple reason that it is one better. Pap is always cranking it up to eleven. I think he took it a little bit personally when people said, "Oh, he can't close every day because he got hurt the year before." He made it a point to prove to everyone the injury was a fluke. Every day of the entire '07 season he was going to take it to eleven. That became evident from our first spring-training conversation.

Talking to guys like Pap, and to most of my teammates, is one of my favorite parts of the job. Baseball is what brought us all together, and it serves as the ultimate glue in any clubhouse. It is always the chief conversation piece. (Although fantasy football does tend to take over once the middle of August rolls around.)

As the monotony of spring training progressed, it was people like Alex Cora, one of our infielders, who would always remind me why I love this game so much. Alex is one of the best teammates I have ever had, and a true friend. As the exhibition season wore on, he would always be up for simply sitting in front of his locker at the far end of the home team's clubhouse and talking. There might have been more than seven months of baseball talk laid out in front of us, but for me and Alex there was no time like the present.

The more you talk to Alex the more you appreciate the player, and person, that he is. I had played against him in college, when he was at the University of Miami, and really didn't like him. And I told him that when we became teammates. "Yeah, I was cocky," he deadpanned. What do they say, "The first sign of addiction is denial"? Well, the mere fact that he wasn't denying that he had a rude personality back then showed me what a stand-up guy he was. And as I got to know him, I realized his character is made up of much more than words.

Living the life of a player who doesn't play every day, like Alex, is not easy. If you're in the major leagues, you usually believe you have the talent to be a starter, but for some it's just not an option. Accepting that is often a difficult proposition. Not only does Alex welcome his role, but he approaches it with the intent that every day is going to be his day in the lineup. Almost every morning that we're on the road, at ten a.m., Alex, Manny Ramirez, our strength and conditioning coach, Dave Page, and I head to the gym. Now, I can understand why Manny and I go; we're playing every day. But Alex doesn't have to, yet he does. And his daily routine goes beyond just a physical preparedness. There is constant video work, and he really analyzes the results. In every respect, he is the type of guy you put your faith in.

Talking with Alex, I am also reminded of my own background. Both of us are bilingual, which can be of enormous value in a big-league clubhouse. But, once again, the major-league present doesn't separate itself from the Mike Lowell past. In other words, I never forget where I came from. Sure, it helps that I can communicate equally as well with Manny Ramirez as with J. D. Drew, and maybe my lack of a language barrier has helped my reputation with others. But for me, it is yet another reminder that what I call my foundation wasn't built just on a ball and a bat.

Despite the fact that both my parents had come from Cuba as eleven-year-olds, they ultimately came around to speaking English as the dominant language in our house. My first words might have been Spanish, and so were many of the sentences that followed all the way up to my school years. But once you get to the classroom, if all the other kids are talking English and nothing else, you soon learn what will get you your turn on the jungle gym, and it's not *"hola."* It was when I started hanging around Bertica's house, where her parents spoke very little English, that my Spanish was taken to a new level. Then came the minor leagues, where I found myself seeking out Spanish reading material and news-casts on television, and, most telling, Spanish-speaking team-mates. And now it's the language I enjoy communicating in the most, partly because it is still something a little bit differ-ent and new.

Speaking both English and Spanish allows me to get to know everyone on the team, which is important given how we are around one another for such an ungodly amount of time. I always thought how unfortunate it was that when you see a team stretching before a game, you would always have the English-speaking guys on one side, and the players who spoke Spanish on the other. An outsider might raise his eyebrows and start whispering about why the two sides aren't together. But I really don't think the division is rooted in any bad feelings; it's more about a comfort level. And most of that has to do with language. Fortunately, I could always stretch in the middle.

Sure, sometimes when I go and talk to the English-speaking guys, the Latin players might say, "Oh, you don't want to talk to us now?" Then I go over to the Latin guys and the English speakers will echo, "Oh, you think you're just a Latino now?" Ribbing is an unavoidable element on a baseball team, so I guess if this was going to be my albatross, it could be worse.

But for me, living a bilingual life will always be an advantage—one that I sometimes feel a little bit selfish about because it has made my life so much easier. But I try to use it to make others' lives a little easier as well. This is important because I think many times things do get lost in translation. There are lots of instances when Latin guys who are coming up through the ranks prefer not talking rather than sounding ignorant. These are proud guys who have overcome a lot and don't want to mess things up with a misplaced word.

One time back in Florida, I remember that Miguel Cabrera, who wasn't even twenty years old when he first arrived in the majors, said in response to a question from the media, "I don't care about the veterans." So the way it comes out is "I'm this young guy who doesn't care about these players who have been in the game a lot longer than I have." But when Miguel explained it in Spanish, it wasn't that he didn't care about the veterans but that he was more concerned about classifying everybody as teammates instead of separating them into factions by age groups. The media didn't care. They ran with what they thought he was saying, not with what his real meaning was. The language divide is a shame, but also a fact of life in every major-league clubhouse. Fortunately, thanks to my unique upbringing, the same thing that is a barrier for some has offered me a kind of bridge.

There was this time when I was playing Single-A ball in Greensboro, North Carolina, and we were going up against the Mets' affiliate. I was playing third base, and there was a guy from the Dominican Republic at the plate, with a runner on first base, and the game was pretty close in the late innings. The third-base coach, who was of Latin descent, went through the set of signs, but the hitter was just staring back like a deer in headlights. He clearly had no idea what the coach was trying to relay to him. I have "Lowell" on the back of my shirt, which obviously doesn't even hint at the notion that I might speak Spanish. So finally, frustrated with his hitter's lack of familiarity with the signs, the coach yelled out, *"Toca,"* the Spanish word for "bunt."

I played it off like I don't know what he was talking about and stayed at normal double-play depth, a few feet from where you would usually position yourself for a bunt. But once the pitcher broke from his set position I started sprinting in, straight at what turned out to be a classic bunt from the batter.

I gathered it in and threw to the second baseman, who relayed it to first for a double play. The coach was standing there befuddled, considering that I was well into my race toward the plate before the batter even hinted at squaring around for the sacrifice. Finally, after the initial shock and with the next batter ready to face the two-out situation, the coach said to me, "You speak Spanish?"

So I responded to him, in Spanish, that I knew every word he was saying and it usually helps when you're born in Puerto Rico. I told him he really should have checked out the roster before the game, because that shows you where everybody is born. He laughed, clearly having learned an unexpected lesson. Unfortunately for him, it was a lesson learned a bit too late—we ended up winning by one run.

Now, years later, the art of talking two languages has gone well beyond sniffing out sacrifice bunts and has led to a flurry of opportunities. Really getting to know my teammates, and passing along the ins and outs of the baseball diamonds, even being able to expand the scope of my trash talking over the Ping-Pong net to Dustin Pedroia. And as I looked across the clubhouse in the final days of the 2007 spring training, with our two new Japanese pitchers, Matsuzaka and Hideki Okajima, being peppered with English lessons, I couldn't help but think what sort of verbal voyage was on their horizon.

As I came to understand as the final days in Fort Myers came and went, this Red Sox team wouldn't be hamstrung by words, with or without my translations.

It was Dice-K and Okie who were now the wide-eyed ones. But after the fourth or fifth time they were invited to dinner with our teammates and kept coming, with or without their translators, I knew we had a connection. This wasn't about flags or United Nations representation. They just liked being around, which, as we were diving into the equivalent of 162 one-day seasons, seemed like half the battle.

CHAPTER TWO

Start of Something Special

Journal entry, April 3, 2007

Opening Day came and went and we got crushed. No worries. If our team stays healthy we will be in the playoffs. After a tough spring (.158), I feel good at the plate. I think I lined out about nine times with only one bloop single. I prefer them catching them in the spring. Want to still have better consistency.

My approach after a Donny talk is to approach more like the minors and early on. Look for MY pitch till two strikes. Middle-in. Remember I can still do damage with two strikes. Feel good about that. We'll see how it translates. I'm closer on the plate. I know I cannot be beat inside.

Spring training had great moments. Alexis learned how to ride a bike without training wheels. She's so coordinated. Took her about forty-five minutes and she fell hard a lot but got right up and now she is just flying around.

Anthony loves his Thomas the Train bike, and with our house at the end of a cul-de-sac it has been great. He's communicating a little better, but still can't pronounce his "l" or "s" well. Hopefully once he gets that he will be a talking machine.

I remember one day when Ozzie Guillen, who is now the manager for the Chicago White Sox but was the Marlins' third-base coach when I was in Florida, pulled me aside in the middle of a series against the Phillies. I was really pressing, trying to do too much, too soon, too well. "I want you," Ozzie said, "to go out and try to hit the ball as soft as possible. Take a regular swing but try and hit it as soft as possible." So I took that approach, and hit a couple of balls right on the money. His simple advice—"you've just got to relax"—turned out to be just what I needed to get over my slump. It was nothing more than making a conscious effort to stay calm and concentrate solely on the five fingers holding the bat. That was it.

It's amazing how easy it is to forget the simplest things in the micromanaged world of baseball.

But by the time I entered the 2007 season, I had somehow allowed Ozzie's lesson to escape me, and I was paying a bit of a price numbers-wise. The year before, I finished the spring hitting .320 and everybody was still asking all of these questions about what ailed me. But this time my numbers were much worse—I was at .150—and there was little question about my potential to produce. There was a confidence in me, a sense that I had cleared one of my career's largest hurdles. This was when I fully realized that the agony of '05 was gone and buried, and in its place was just the simple day-to-day analysis that came with preparing for the upcoming '07 campaign.

Just before opening the season in Kansas City, we played two exhibition games in Philadelphia, and in the visiting manager's office they had an enormous chart showing everybody's spring-training batting averages. I walked in and Tito about fell on the floor laughing, pointing at the ".150" next to my name.

"I can't believe you hit .150," he said. I told him he was preaching to the converted. I felt like I hadn't gotten a hit in about two weeks. Part of this was because in the spring you only get a couple of at-bats each game and then head home. But the other part was that I *hadn't* gotten a hit in about two weeks.

"How do you feel?" Tito asked. I knew I felt a whole lot better than ".150." A bloop hit every once in a while would have been nice, but I had gone through a stretch of line outs and the like.

Turned out, Tito agreed. "That's perfect!" he exclaimed. "You want all of those line outs and bad bounces to take place in the spring. That's what it's all about." I started to feel better.

I began to think maybe I should be holding my head up a bit higher as we dove into the regular season.

It was around the time the real games got under way that I finally remembered Ozzie's advice. Just make good contact, because until they put a steering wheel on the ball, you can't control anything after that. Ball down the middle, hit it back up the middle. A pitch inside, turn on it. Outside, go the other way. Nothing more, nothing less. The Wiffle ball way of doing things was serving me well once again. It was simply a matter of bringing the perforated plastic to the forefront of my psyche.

I probably ended up having three sessions with the Sox mental performance coach, Donny Kalkstein, throughout the '07 season, compared to about ten the year before. But every single get-together with him left an indelible mark on me. For instance, back in '06, we were playing Minnesota, and I was struggling. He said, "Do you remember in April, when you were telling me how comfortable you were feeling? Why don't we get back to that point?" Exactly. Why don't we? It seemed simple enough.

"Well, let's break it down. How are you feeling now?" Donny asked. I brought up the issue of public perception and told him about how in spring training I had decided to stop reading the Web sites and newspapers because of the negativity. That spawned another question: Should I check out those places when things were good, or would that be sort of hypocritical? "By all means," he said. "Read every single article about yourself when you do well." For me, however, it wasn't that simple. Vanity isn't really my thing, and that seemed a little bit vain.

"No way," Donny continued. "If you look at it as vain it's going to be vain. But if you look at it this way—as the more sentences you put in those stories, the better your results have been and will be—then that's what you will remember. You should read the articles because they're going to say, 'Mike Lowell turned on a two-two pitch,' and then it puts you in the mind frame to think, 'What did I do on that two-two pitch?' All those nuggets are positive nuggets. Put them in your brain; put them in your back pocket."

So I went back to the Web sites and newspapers, and believe it or not that is what ultimately got me to a point where I was suddenly comfortable with where I was with my swing and approach. Now, if I wanted to read an article about the Red Sox, I read it. I didn't care about the consequences, because the negativity wasn't going to hold me down. I was at a place mentally that was so much more advanced than where I had been.

Still, I had my superstitions; virtually all baseball players do.

It had got to the point where if I had a good game and I urinated in the second stall, I would go urinate in the second stall the next day because I believed that would allow me to have a good game. But when I told Donny about this he disapproved: "What's more important? Urinating in the second stall or all the drill work you do before the game? You're devaluing all your hard work by thinking your success is based on a bathroom stall." And when he put it that simply, I woke up and realize how stupid I had been.

Just to prove the point, I made sure I urinated in a different stall every day, no matter how I had done in the previous night's game. I was going to urinate anywhere I damn well wanted.

But I have to admit, it is a little different when it comes to the team. If we're winning, I may do things like keep putting on my shoes in the same way. What can I say? Old habits are hard to break. But when it comes to me personally, I was now convinced that my achievement came not from any routines but from the work ethic and preparation I put forth. I would determine my own success. That was a big adjustment for me and it made a world of difference heading into '07. (Even if I had the occasional inkling that the American League East standings were riding on my shoes and socks.)

Superstitions will always be part of the lifeblood of base-ball, but now I only called upon them for the sake of the team.

My mind was in the right place, but I still ended up striking out in my very first at-bat of '07, against Royals' starter Gil Meche. Thankfully it would be two weeks before I fanned again, and after the first eighty at-bats, I had struck out only four times. I was never really the kind of player who swung and missed a whole bunch, but my new stats were very en-couraging. It was April and I was in a good place. That's a nice feeling when you have at least five more months of potential self-doubt ahead.

By the middle of the first month, it was clear that this might be the best team I had ever played on, and that the season to come could very well turn out to be a classic one. This excitement reached a peak on April 22, with the Yankees in town for one of those be-all and end-all, there's-only-140-games-left-in-the-season type of ESPN Sunday-night showdowns.

Feeding the excitement was the unexpected division standings. We knew we were a really good team, so our residence in first place wasn't all that shocking. But what did cause a double take was the Yankees' struggles. We couldn't believe it. Our feeling was that they were probably just a bit off, but still too good not to make a run. So we vowed to do everything we could to keep the pressure on. If this team—our biggest rivals and baseball's biggest payroll—kept collapsing, fine, but none of us really believed, with their track records, that was going to happen. And it didn't.

But the April 22 game was not a happy one for Yankees fans. The Yankees got off to a 3–0 lead with their rookie pitcher, Chase Wright, taking his turn in the Sunday-night spotlight. But then Manny Ramirez led off the third inning with a blast. Okay, we were on the board. Even before the home run we felt momentum was on our side, having won the first two games of the series and eleven of our first sixteen games. But then, four pitches later, J. D. Drew laid into one that went out over the center-field fence. The air was thickening with excitement, which is common at Fenway Park, but usually not this early in a game, even with the Yanks in town.

Now it was my turn. You tend to get a bit geared up when the guy in front of you hits a home run, because your first inclination is to do the same thing. It always looks like it feels so good. So I was consciously playing down my own expectations, telling myself, "Just stay within yourself, and put in a good swing. Just put in a good swing, that's all." If it was as easy to hit home runs as simply repeating the joyous moment of the player in front of you, everyone would be hitting home runs every time. If it feels good, do it, right? It wasn't that simple—never is.

The third pitch from Wright was a changeup down in the strike zone. I stayed on it and crushed it. There are precious few hits over the course of a season that you just know are going over the wall once ball meets bat. This was one of those. It was also one of the few instances when I was going to make it a point to enjoy the home-run trot. Three home runs in a row, we had just tied the game, and it was a Sunday-night game against the Yankees. That kind of April drama doesn't come around all that often, especially in the third inning, so when it does there is no crime in smelling the roses a bit.

I went back to the dugout, still soaking in each high five and fan-induced wave of emotion, when Coco Crisp, our center fielder, told me, "You've got to sit next to me. Manny sat next to me. Then J.D. sat next to me, and now you've got to sit next to me." No problem. Right on cue, second pitch to Jason Varitek, another home run over the left-field wall. Four home runs in a row! I had never seen that, in T-ball, Little League, minors, majors, nowhere. Honestly it felt as if we had won the

World Series. That was the kind of unbridled chaos that ensued in our dugout. For once our level of enthusiasm was equal to, or greater than, that of the fans.

There are two newspapers I had framed since my arrival in Boston. The "I Hope He Dies!" from the *Boston Herald*, relaying my thoughts on Fidel Castro, and the one with the four home-run hitters from that night all pictured on the front of the sports page. I got signatures from each of us on the page, because, let's face it, that's probably something we'll never see again. And against the Yankees! It almost sounds like a movie, it's such a perfect script.

And, as I discovered later, it only got better.

The eventual 7–6 win over the Yankees turned into an even more defining evening for me after I hit another home run in the seventh, a three-run blast that gave us the lead for good. But it was something that happened the next day that I will always remember. Sarah Stevenson, who works for the Red Sox's community relations department, asked me to sign a shirt for a girl named Courtney Butcher, who had recently passed away. I couldn't understand why the family would want this. "She was a huge Red Sox fan," said Sarah, "a big Mike Lowell fan, and they want to put it by the coffin." That blew me away. I didn't know what to do, what to write. All I could think of was "Courtney. May God be with you. Rest in peace."

Then more information started to trickle in. Courtney had been killed in a car accident the Friday before, and she'd had tickets to Sunday night's game against the Yankees. Her seats were supposed to be on top of the left-field wall, or the Green Monster, right in the vicinity where I hit the third of the four third-inning home runs. In the coming days I discovered that ESPN's Jon Miller, who was calling the game, said, "That one is going all the way to New Hampshire." As I came to learn, Courtney had been a student at the University of New Hampshire.

Later in the season, I finally had the opportunity to meet Courtney's family on the Fenway Park field before our August 14 game with Tampa Bay. The game unfolded, with most of the attention focused on our starting pitcher, Jon Lester, who was making his first home appearance since being diagnosed with cancer almost exactly a year before. Jon pitched superbly, but we still found ourselves in a 1–0 hole entering the ninth inning. I came to the plate with one out, against the Tampa Bay closer Al Reyes, and as I came to find out later, Courtney's father, Jim Butcher, then looked to the sky and said, "Courtney, we need one from your guy right here." On the third pitch I hit one over the wall to tie the game. Three batters later, Coco singled in Jason Varitek with the game-winning run.

After I found out what Jim had said, I couldn't help but think about how so often it seems like we're all connected, like in the movie *Crash*. It also made me think about what a powerful effect I have on others as a major-league baseball player in Boston. When somebody comes up to me and says something like, "My son loves you!" I generally don't feel like I'm deserving of that praise. But I have to respect it. My kids are a bit too young for that kind of thing now, but if they ever look up to somebody famous—other than Mickey Mouse—I really hope that whoever it is takes the same approach that I try to. The way I see it, if somebody is going to put me on a pedestal, it's my responsibility to be a good guy and give validation to the fact that they placed me up there.

When I was a kid, I had four posters on my wall (not including a ceiling full of Michael Jordan posters). There were Mike Schmidt, Jose Canseco, Pete Rose, and Don Mattingly. I thought Mattingly was a good player, but I was more drawn to him because Channel 2 in Miami carried some of the Yankees' games. If cable was around, Don might not have made the cut. Canseco was a homegrown guy who had done well, and Schmidt had me in the fold since I had gotten his Burger King baseball card, which also helped lead me to his then Phillies teammate, Rose.

I would eventually get to meet Schmidt and Rose, and during the '03 World Series, Mattingly came up and asked me to sign a ball for his kid. "Excuse me," I said. "You want me to sign a ball for Preston? No, no, no. You need to sign a ball for me first." I was totally taken aback that this guy I had stared at up on my wall all those years was now asking me for an autograph. And I don't really know Canseco, having only met him briefly when he was at my charity golf tournament. But Jose was very cordial and accommodating to everybody who wanted a picture or an autograph. It was the same when I met Rose, with whom I had the time of my life signing autographs at a memorabilia store in Cooperstown, New York. So I wanted to be like those guys, to be a role model for my young fans like they had been to me.

One of the first times I fully realized the power of my position as an athlete in the public eye was during an appearance for the Marlins at a Miami-area Cuban cafeteria. People were in line, and I was signing away, when I saw this grandmotherly lady crying. It was all-out bawling, the kind of crying you see at Michael Jackson concerts. I was a bit stunned, not having a clue as to what was going on. Finally she came up to me and said, "You know, my grandson had cancer just like you, and he said that if you made it through, he can make it through." Oh my goodness. What do you say to that?

I was taken off guard, totally off guard, but it was a wake-up call. I knew right then that no matter how daunting it was, I had to recognize the impact I had and do my best to be a good role model.

All of the attention and adoration that comes with the job, some people view it as negative. But when someone like that grandmother comes up and tells you something like that, how can you think it's anything but a positive? It's a weird dynamic, for sure, but the key is staying grounded and true to the things you believed in before you had the money or stepped on the big stage. The bottom line is that admiration is sure better than the alternative. But with all the adulation comes responsibility.

By the end of April '07, we were playing well, I was hitting well, and I was starting to really feel at home with the Red

Sox. I was happy. But one bit of negativity did cast a shadow on my early-season euphoria.

In 2005 I had won the Gold Glove for National League third basemen, given to the best defensive player at the position. A year later I made six errors all season. But in '07 I made three miscues in our second game of the season, and then, in a late-April game at Yankee Stadium, two more came. May was on our doorstep and I had eight errors. This I wasn't used to.

I had been a good fielder pretty much all my life, partially just because of the hands I had been blessed with. Playing second base, I made only two errors my senior year. One was when I came in to pitch, went to pick a guy off at first, and short-hopped the throw. The other was sheer ego: I scooped a tough shot, hotdogged it a bit, and threw one into the dirt in front of the first baseman. That play has always stuck in my mind, reminding me that you have to stay on top of every single play, every single time.

Maybe the worst stretch, up until April of 2007, that I ever had in the field was when my position went from amateur second baseman to professional third baseman. Up until I started collecting paychecks for playing, I had never manned third base in my life. And it showed. When I began at the hot corner, I tried to basically play the position like I would at shortstop or second base, going at the ball every time. I had failed to learn that this spot on the diamond screamed out for a reactive approach, not the proactive method I was familiar with. The result was more than twenty-four errors in about seventy-two games. Needless to say, defense was no longer a walk in the park for me.

I remember there was this guy who wrote online minor-league reports for the New York teams, the Mets and Yankees, and somebody told me if you go to this particular site, every single player in these organizations was rated and categorized. There was "Cup of coffee," "Chance to be in the big leagues in a couple of years," "A regular in the big leagues," "Budding superstar," or "No chance." This was my first introduction to the Internet, and it was also the start of my reluctance to dive into this world of negativity.

I looked at what it said about me: "Mike Lowell, Oneonta Yankees, an abomination at third base." I couldn't understand where this hatred came from. This guy was saying I was a third baseman with no power who couldn't field.

The perception became clearer one day in Oneonta when one of the thousand fans in attendance decided to make his feelings known. I had a terrible game, making a couple of errors to go with an 0-for-3 outing at the plate. After all of this, I heard this distinct New York accent, "Lowell! Lowell!" I turned and our eyes met. "You are a horror. A horror to the game of baseball. A horror, I tell you." I'll never forget that to the day I die.

Changing this perception became a priority.

My arm was plenty strong enough, so I decided the first step in altering the cyberspace opinion was to take a few ground balls, some more ground balls, and then a bunch of extra grounders. I had to start understanding the angles of playing third base, which I realized was perhaps the most important aspect of the position. I wasn't going to get any faster, but I could make those first few steps a whole lot more effective.

The next year, in Greensboro, I made thirty-five errors, but over 136 games, and the following season there were twenty-three miscues in about the same number of contests. I knew I was making progress, and I allowed that some of the errors could be chalked up to the inconsistencies that come with playing on minor-league fields. My hands were finally finding themselves in the right spot, and, as I have discovered, for a third baseman that is almost everything.

By the time I became a Triple-A third baseman, I had an official goal for myself: to finish a season with under ten errors. Under double digits just sounded good. An infield coach in the minors told me that an average third baseman in the big leagues makes over fifteen errors. That seemed like such a big number to me. I knew I could be better than average.

By the time I became an everyday major-league third baseman with Florida, I was confident that my single-digit goal was more than attainable in any season going forward. In 2000 I made twelve errors, but the next year I hit it with nine. Since then, up until '07, I had entered double digits just one time, with back-to-back six-error seasons in '05 and '06. I believed I had become a good third baseman, proving wrong the Internet "abomination" talk of the early years. What I didn't realize until years into my third-base existence was exactly how good my numbers had become.

One day, in one of my final years with the Marlins, some of us were having a conversation about defense, when one of the writers who covered the team asked me if I knew what the National League record was for the fewest errors by a third baseman in a season. I thought it was probably around four, but he said it was eight. I said that couldn't be, because I had made seven the previous season. "You did?" he said. "I've got to look into that." He did and what he found was that I had the highest fielding percentage in the history of the game for any third baseman. Second was Brooks Robinson. Brooks Robinson, the preeminent example for defensive excellence at the third-base position! You can often slant statistics whichever way you want to make a point, but I was buying this one. Anytime you can say you went from being called a defensive liability to the best of all time, you've got to soak that in.

Winning the Gold Glove was also a nice bit of affirmation, but I was especially pleased knowing that I hadn't let my woes with the bat that season affect my performance on the field. When you're young, it's hard to keep the two things, hitting and fielding, separate in your mind. You can be thinking about how you didn't get a hit with a pitch you really should have crushed, and then before you know it you've made an error because you were still stewing about it with a glove on your hand.

And as good as I was with the glove in '05, in my estimation '06 was even better. The grounds crew at Fenway Park is great, but it is an older stadium and you don't have that nice, thin Bermuda grass where you rarely get a bad hop. You are forced to play balls a lot differently at Fenway than you would on other fields. So the fact that I had made just six errors *on this field*, that I had proved the doubters wrong *on this field*, was the icing on the cake.

Maybe there is some minor leaguer out there who has been scarred by the Internet experts and can look at my path for some peace of mind. For me all it took was a few extra grounders, some hard work, and some common sense.

Believing you have it figured out, however, can be just as dangerous, as I discovered after making my seventh and eighth errors under the Yankee Stadium late-April sun.

Eight errors in one month! The frustrating part of the final two was that one of them, a ball hit by Derek Jeter, was a routine grounder simply popping out of my glove. There was an easy explanation, but it was difficult to digest. Four straight seasons I had used the same Wilson A2000 glove in virtually all my games and it had served me well. I had another glove, but I had only broken it in for use in batting practice. But after replaying the two Yankee Stadium errors over and over in my head, I decided it was time for a change. For the next game, I chose to promote my backup glove to game duty. I saw it as the end of one era and the beginning of another. What was the worst I could do, make more errors?

For some this might seem like an inconsequential move, switching from one baseball glove to another. But for me this was big. The piece of leather has to feel like an extension of your hand, willing to hold the ball tight upon first introduction and ready to release once it is time for the transfer. The

Wilson I was kicking to the curb had served me well for almost seven hundred straight games, guiding me through a World Series championship, a Gold Glove award, and the transition to a challenging new home field. In all this time it had taken off one inning—just one—to defer to its backup. I kept thinking of those three outs, though. They were enough to convince me that my number-two glove was ready for prime-time status.

When I play defense, I honestly want them to hit me the ball every single time. They say that the time you don't want it hit to you is when it's going to be hit to you, but I always want the ball because that part of the game is fun for me. But on August 13, 2006, I entered foreign territory. For maybe the first time in my entire big-league career I didn't want the ball coming anywhere near me. When you're using the equivalent of a Triple-A glove on a big-league stage during the most tension-filled moment, trepidation is understandable.

We were carrying a four-run lead over Baltimore heading into the home half of the eighth inning. The half inning before, a string on my "gamer" glove had broken, and it was enough of a problem that even Jim Rowe, our trainer, who is pretty adept at fixing those sorts of problems, couldn't get it ready by the time we took the field for the ninth. But I was thinking that with a four-run lead, and our All-Star closer, Jonathan Papelbon, ready to put out any potential fire, an unfamiliar fielding implement shouldn't really be a concern. So, for almost the first time since the beginning of 2003, I walked out into a major-league baseball game with a different A2000.

Before I knew it, I was standing at third base with our lead cut to two and Orioles runners at every base. I realized I should want the ball hit to me in this spot, and have always embraced that philosophy of fielding, but this time I wanted it to go somewhere else.

I should have known better.

The count went full on Baltimore batter Melvin Mora, a right-handed hitter who usually takes the kind of healthy stroke that keeps third basemen on their toes. Then, on the ninth pitch of the at-bat, Mora scorched a hot grounder down the third-base line. I took a couple of quick steps toward the chalk and backhanded the ball, temporarily forgetting that the leather I was counting on to embrace the smash was still a virgin. But the glove did what it was supposed to do, and I followed suit, reaching in, grabbing the sphere, and throwing it across the diamond for the game's final out. It was a long toss, but when your glove executes its part of the equation flawlessly, the sense of security usually carries over to the throw.

I knew switching gloves heading into the season's second month wasn't going to be the cure-all when it came to improving upon my eight-error opening month, but I also thought that my defensive game was still pretty strong, despite what some were saying. The bottom line was that I had to start figuring how to better handle the position's most prevalent pitfall—the in-between hop. A lot of times you are getting right-handed hitters who get on top of the ball and supply a healthy amount of topspin. With a shortstop you have more time to let the hit (and the spin) play out, but at third there has to be a respect for a potential bunt, so you have no choice but to play closer. The problem was, in April I seemed to be getting caught in between a lot more than I had in previous months.

Over the course of a season you have about eight occasions when you close your eyes, try to put your chest in front of the ball, and hope it hits you and falls in front of your body quickly enough for you to throw the guy out. But in that first month of the '07 season, I felt like I got about fifteen of them. It led me to the video room, where I tried to identify whether I was standing in the same spot as previous years, which, as it turned out, I was. Frustration, and errors, be damned, I decided that riding out the stretch of bad fortune was the only tactic to take. It was. I ended up with fifteen errors, a career high. But considering where I had come from, it was a number I could deal with. As I've learned throughout my life, experiencing setbacks makes the achievements that follow that much sweeter.

While I was trying to figure this all out, my teammate Dustin Pedroia was staring down his own baseball demons, and learning many of the same lessons I had when digging myself out from '05. Dustin was our rookie second baseman, having taken over the starting role from Mark Loretta, who left for Houston via free agency. Dustin is a guy who befuddled many of the professional talent evaluators, standing five foot six with a swing befitting a man twice his size. If he failed in his first full season, people were going to say, "I told you so." In his first thirty-one games, serving as a late-season call-up in

'06, he hit .191, and that was followed by an unappetizing .182 in the first month of '07. The vultures were circling, but I had a feeling Dustin was going to evade them.

Dustin and I clicked from day one, although I'm not entirely sure why. I knew he was better than his average showed in '06. His at-bats were good. If you can possibly hit a hard .191, he did it for those six weeks. But I think the main reason we got along so well was that I could relate to the chip he had on his shoulder. His chip was there because of his stature and because of the hesitancy by some to classify him as a good player. I know from experience that a chip isn't a bad thing. What do you think was resting next to my head after being told I wasn't good enough to play varsity in high school, getting drafted in the twentieth round, dealing with cancer, and all those other obstacles that came my way? It's good to have a chip; it brings out the best in you. It also shows exactly how much you truly believe in yourself, and nobody believes in himself more than Dustin. You doubt him, he's going to make you pay the price.

When he first came up in '06, he wasn't in good shape, having been hurt for much of the season. But that gave me the perfect opening to see where this kid was at. I kept teasing him: "They told me you were a second-rounder. I didn't know they drafted short, fat people that early. If I knew that, I would have just not grown and ate a lot of cheeseburgers." Sure enough, he dropped twenty-five pounds and came into camp in great condition. But the cockiness never stops with Dustin. We were in Cleveland, where there is a Ping-Pong table just outside the clubhouse, and he came in and challenged me to a best-of-five match. I don't want to toot my own horn, but I'm a pretty good Ping-Pong player. So I literally beat him twenty-eight straight games. I started to get a little bored so I began to mess around with him a little bit, letting "Petie" get out to a big lead before he finally won, 24–22. He was now one and twenty-eight against me, but that didn't stop Dustin. He immediately ran into the clubhouse and started yelling, "Who's the champ?"

I said, "What if you went oh for twenty-eight at the plate and got a hit? You'd still be pretty upset. Don't give me any of that crap."

So just to bring Petie back down to earth, Tito came in and started making fun of him, saying things like, "What? Did they have to cut the legs off the table for you to play?" That, along with a few more losses, set him off again. But we love him, man. When you have a guy come into the dugout after hitting his second major-league home run, like he did against Toronto's A. J. Burnett at the end of the '06 season, and start yelling, "Ninety-six [miles per hours] coming in, a hundred ninety-six going out!" well, that's priceless. Sure, I usually enjoy firing back, "Simmer down, Napoleon." But I love it.

It showed us that this guy had the kind of passion it was going to take to fight his way out of his April hitting woes. He just put these bad memories behind him, and with the American League Rookie of the Year award handed him in November, he buried them completely.

I thought it was fitting that Dustin turned around his season, and many of the nonbelievers, in a game against one of the big league's best pitchers, Johan Santana. Petie would have had every excuse to either sit or fail when Tito put him in the lineup on May 5 against Santana. He was hitting .180, and Alex Cora was playing lights-out at second base. But thanks to a small adjustment he learned from our hitting coach, Dave Magadan, in which Dustin simply moved the position of his head, Petie came out and ripped off two hits that day. Guaranteed 0 for 4? Pedroia was having none of it. He wanted to play all the time, and then some more. He even played the final two months of the season with a cracked bone in his left hand. Pure Pedroia.

Not much came easy for Petie, and maybe that's why we get along so well. We both can appreciate a life without shortcuts. Perhaps that's also a bond we both share with the people who have invested themselves, and their money, into following this team. It's not easy getting tickets, near impossible for some. But they find a way, and that isn't lost on either of us, with our never-say-die natures.

For example, one time before game one in the playoff series with the Angels, Petie and his wife, Kelli, went out to eat with Bertica and me at this Mexican place called La Verdad right near Fenway. Anyway, it started pouring rain outside. I mean, in the time it took me to run across the street after parking my car, I was soaked. So we were in there drying off when Kelli told us she just saw a bunch of people waiting in the downpour to get tickets for the game. *In this rain?* I thought. To me that was almost incomprehensible. So this struck a chord with all of us, but especially my wife.

When we're in New York, Bertica is always asking for $20 bills to give to the people asking for money. I'm like, "You know some of those people are just going to buy alcohol with it, and you'll be adding fuel to the fire." But she is always quick to respond, "Yeah, but what about the one who is going to buy food?" She is always my conscience, and this time was no different.

"We've got to take those people food," Bertica said. Petie and I looked out the window again and agreed this was the right thing to do. We ordered a half dozen entrées and a bunch of chips and stuff like that and headed over. By the time we got there it had stopped raining, but we were still intent on delivering the food and hopefully getting in and out without any media fanfare. "Hey," I said upon arriving on the stretch of sidewalk filled with rain-soaked, weary-looking bodies, "are you guys waiting for tickets?" A chorus of loud Boston accents erupted: "It's Pedroia! It's Lowell!" A camera guy heard this and started running over with his equipment, so I told Petie we had to get out of there. But the next day the newspaper talked to somebody who was out there, and so word of the incident got out. A buddy of mine called and said, "Good PR move." That upset me. We didn't do it for the publicity; we did it because of our appreciation.

The way we looked at it, we knew what it was like to be sitting out in the rain, sleeping on the sidewalk. But we had been rewarded for our perseverance, so why shouldn't they?

I wanted to give something back to the fans. I guess it's

my way of expressing my love for baseball, for this game that my father introduced me to so many years ago.

I remember the first time I played the sport as a three-year-old in the backyard of my family's house on Santurce Avenue in Coral Gables. My dad bounced the ball to me and I threw it back. And when my father wasn't around, a wall of the house would have to suffice. That was it. I was hooked. I could throw a ball against a wall for hours. For my parents, that was the first clue.

Then came T-ball, and there is the image of Dad again, always stepping up to show me the right way to play. I can still recall being a six-year-old shortstop in T-ball and having the thoughts run through my head: *Runner on first, so if the ball is hit to me, we're trying to get the out at second.* Even then, it wasn't just about fielding the ball; it was about what we were going to do once that ball was fielded. And those thoughts didn't just pop into my head. They were Dad's influence.

There was no cable television, so I always looked forward to Saturdays because that meant the Game of the Week was going to be on, and Dad would be sitting right there with me, not so much teaching me the game but just talking baseball. I really loved all sports, but something about baseball called out to me more than the others. Again, that was probably because of Dad.

To understand me it is probably best to get a handle on the makings of my father, the man they call Carlos. Before me, he was the baseball player of the family, and, in some people's eyes, he still is. When Dad landed in Puerto Rico after leaving Cuba at age eleven, he immediately made an impression. He was becoming more of a man, growing with each experience, and his talents on the baseball field were following suit, particularly on the pitching mound. In a few years Dad's talents were on display at San Ignacio High School, where he earned an academic scholarship from St. Joseph's University in Philadelphia. True to form for our family, there was no free ride when it came to playing baseball at St. Joe's. Dad had to walk on to the team. But two years later he was MVP, and one more season after that came a no-hitter.

Before graduating from St. Joe's, he decided to head back to Puerto Rico for dental school. That's when Dad found himself back in the baseball community he had left behind four years earlier, and this led him to a spot on the Puerto Rican National Team's roster. His first test was the 1970 World Series of Amateur Baseball, which included such players as the longtime Dodger pitcher Burt Hooton. Exam passed. In Dad's only start he beat Venezuela with fourteen strikeouts. A year later, the tournament came around again, except this time my father was faced with an entirely unique challenge—it was to be held in the place his family had left behind nearly ten years earlier, Cuba.

Dad went back to his former home, fending off memories of the hardships left behind, and became the tournament's only pitcher to win three games. In twenty-seven innings he allowed just one earned run, although it still wasn't good enough to circumvent the Cuban way of doing things, as the award for the tournament's top pitcher went to one of the hosts' hurlers. In my father's eyes this was predictable, but it still left a bad taste in his mouth.

But he was proud of his performance on the mound. And when he went up against Italy—a team my father said you could throw in a blender and still come away with barely one legitimate baseball player—Dad tossed a shutout while supplying the game's only run via an opposite-field home run. But his glow of victory didn't last long. After the 1–0 win the Puerto Rican team was getting ready to load onto its bus when Fidel Castro requested to shake the hands of all the players in his private box. One Puerto Rican player, my father, chose to wait behind for the rest of his team on the bus. He was not about to acknowledge the man who spearheaded a government that persecuted my father's family and friends and committed unspeakable atrocities. Shaking the hand of this man would have been another black cloud among the memories my father's family was so desperately trying to put behind them.

That refusal to shake Castro's hand has always stayed with me. My father stood up for what he believed in, and because of it I have always tried to do the same.

Dad got another crack at exacting a measure of revenge against Castro in '72 when he went back to Cuba to pitch in a tournament called, ironically enough, the Friendly Series. This time my father went face-to-face against his former countrymen, the Cuban National Team. He went seven innings, leaving with a 5–1 lead, having scored the fifth run to complement his extraordinary pitching performance. That final run would prove to be the winning run in what ended up a 5–4 Puerto Rico victory. My father had become the first Cuban to ever come back and beat the Cuban National League team.

Dad stood on the field, soaked in tears. Ever since leaving for Puerto Rico, he had dreamed of this moment, and here it was. Outside corners had been hit. A changeup he almost never threw for strikes had been used successfully upward of twenty times. Someone was on Dad's side that day. It was the highlight of an extraordinary athletic career.

Of course, Castro wouldn't acknowledge the historic ramifications of the former Cuban pitcher's performance, pointing out that Dad wasn't truly a native of the Communist country, having been born in California. But Castro knew. Everybody knew. For my family, it was, and will always be, a good measure of sweet, sweet justice.

Dad kept pitching and playing, sometimes to my mother's dismay. In February of 1974, I was due to be born, but my due date was at the same time that my father was supposed to be flying to the Dominican Republic to pitch in the Central American Caribbean Games. The decision was made that Mom would be induced so that Dad could make the games, which he did, pitching Puerto Rico to two of their victories. My father literally went straight from the delivery room to the airport. Ask any member of my family, and they will tell you: It was at that moment that I was predestined to live the life of a baseball player. A lot has transpired during my journey from the womb to the World Series, but, evidently, my father had already set in motion the entire path when he called for that cab back on February 24, 1974.

Dad wouldn't talk about how good he was, but others filled me in. Even in the minor leagues, all kinds of coaches from Puerto Rico would see my last name and immediately ask if I was a relative of Carlos Lowell. After they heard he was my father, they would go on and on about how good he was. I would then call home and tell him these guys, with whom he had shared the same love of the game in Puerto Rico, were singing his praises. "You see, I wasn't lying to you all of these years," he would say with a chuckle. I always appreciated listening to Dad talk baseball, but once I began to understand I was listening to Carlos Lowell, the Puerto Rican baseball-playing hero, I saw him in a new light.

Dad's life eventually transitioned from the baseball field to his dentist office, but his kids always gave him a connection to the game he loved. The great thing, for us all, was that he only worked a half day on Wednesdays. That was always the best day. From two thirty to four thirty in the afternoon he was all ours.

From the time I was six years old and all the way up until high school, my brothers and I would head to the Epiphany Elementary School field with my dad—and a bat and a bucket of about fifty balls. There was only one rule: When Dad threw batting practice we had to swing at every pitch. There was no time to be picky and choosy. And you know what? Until I got into pro ball, I never had a batting-practice pitcher who was better than my father, not even in college. After everybody had their turn hitting, usually about two buckets of balls per batter, Dad would hit some grounders and a few superhigh pop-ups just to see if we could catch them.

It only got better when all the balls had been hit and throws had been made. We picked up all the balls, went straight to 7-Eleven, and got Slurpees. That was the reward. Wednesdays were always the best. And it wasn't only because of the bonding and frozen fruity drinks.

The afternoons also allowed for valuable time with my older brother, Carlos. We were separated by less than two years, and shared a room for much of our childhood. And it was during that time together, both at home and on the baseball field, when Carlos helped show me the importance of responsibility. He never talked down to me, or at me, but only to me. Carlos laid the groundwork for all of us kids, and for that I was, and will always be, grateful.

Those were the times when I learned to play the game, and act, the right way. I learned what it meant to work hard. Like I said, Wednesday will always be my favorite day of the week.

Because I always played one age level up in organized baseball—for instance, if I was eight, I would play with the nines and tens—I was able to keep a bit of that Wednesday-afternoon feeling of playing with my dad and older brother. Having my dad as my first coach gave me so many priceless moments that still ring through my head. I remember, for instance, the first time I dove for a ball, and he yelled, "That's the way you do it. If you're going to play, it's got to be as hard as you can all the time." Even the way my father interacted with other kids, some who really weren't that good, impressed me greatly. I knew what it was like to be successful, and he wanted to give those players that same feeling of accomplishment. A kid would make a simple catch, but my dad immediately turned that into a "great" catch. Dad was praising them, but teaching me.

I'm sure there were parents who simply dropped off their kids at baseball practice to get rid of them for three hours. Dad took on the responsibility to make sure those kids had a good time. It all came back to treating people the right way. You don't have to be the best player to be treated the right way. There are no small roles in baseball.

I remember when I was with the Yankees, there were guys like Tim Raines, Luis Sojo, and Chili Davis, who, at the time, were all on the bench (as the fourth outfielder, backup infielder, and designated hitter, respectively). In spring training we would all find ourselves in the dugout quite a bit, watching the regulars. And even though it wasn't us out there, we would always be talking about the game playing out in front of us, analyzing it, saying things like, "This guy, he will never double up on a fastball after throwing the first pitch for a strike." Because not only are there no small roles in baseball, there are no small details. Imagine, these guys probably had forty years of service time between them, and they were still looking into every nook and cranny the game had to offer. That's where you learn the game. We all want to win and be good players, but without the attention to each tiny facet, that isn't going to happen.

Thankfully, Dad never forced his love for the game on me—which is probably why I ended up loving it so much. It was never a matter of a father living vicariously through his son, although I would hope that the sight of me standing on Coors Field with the World Series MVP trophy might offer a bit of that. Dad had already had his experiences, and he simply wanted to put me in the best position possible to have my own, whatever or wherever they might be.

I played volleyball, I played soccer, and I played basketball growing up, and my dad was there for every single game, no matter the sport. Not to yell, instruct, or scream at me after the final whistle was blown, but simply to support. In eighth grade I hit a phase that would have torn up many with my father's background, but only fortified the kind of parent he was. I didn't want to play baseball anymore. I needed a break from the game. So what did my father—the baseball hero from Puerto Rico and role model for all of the neighborhood's aspiring ballplayers—say? "All right, don't play. But you're not sitting around the house. You're doing something." I did do something. I played baseball, but only because I rediscovered the love for the game, not because my father made me. I didn't know it, but that moment was a test, and we both passed with flying colors.

Sure, I have fended off a fair number of slings and arrows along the way to living out my dream as a member of the Boston Red Sox, but I am also unbelievably fortunate. I've had every opportunity, and I owe much of it to my father, who set me on this path.

Take, for example, the time when, as an eight-year-old, I was invited to join a group of nine- and ten-year-olds in going

to Japan to play in a tournament. Now, this was the first time
I had ever left my house, let alone the country, and my parents
weren't even going to go with me. There was a travel agent
mix-up and the trip was going to cost around $7,000 per per-
son, so there was no way anybody else in my family could
make the trip. Needless to say, my mom was totally against it.
She said, "You're sending the kid halfway around the world at
eight years old? He doesn't even know his own street." But
Dad stepped in and reminded Mom that some of his best experiences were those when he went away with teams. Those,
he reiterated, were the memories you never forget and can
never be replaced. He knew.

As a ten-year-old my father had gone from one side of
Cuba, the capital of Havana, to the other, Oriente, for a youth
baseball tournament, a trip that was just over eight hundred
kilometers but might as well have been a world away. His first
game was in the Cuban side of Guantánamo Bay, where he
was greeted by the first field he ever played on without a hint
of grass. It was nothing more than black dirt. My father's team
would win that game, and every other of the contests facing
them on the trip. Those victories offered happy memories as
the years went by, but my dad's biggest impression of the journey wouldn't come until years later.

While Dad was playing in Cuba for Puerto Rico in 1971, a
man approached him and handed him a photo that had been
torn from a yearbook. It pictured a boy in a baseball uniform.
The man told my father that the boy in the picture had played
against Dad in the youth tournament. Pictures of all the players

competing in the '71 championship had been published and spread throughout Cuba, and the man recognized my dad's face from years before. It was an improbable twist of fate that would have never come to pass if not for a ten-year-old's introduction to cross-country travel. Dad understood the value of going to Japan. And you know what? He was right. I went to Japan and I will never forget it, even though we got absolutely killed. I mean decimated. There was some miscommunication and we ended up playing eleven- and twelve-year-olds. But it was still worth it.

All my childhood experiences and education were paying off as we ventured further into the 2007 season. I was playing well and the Red Sox were entrenched in first place. But as I had come to learn over the course of my life, adversity rarely takes too long a vacation.

CHAPTER THREE

The Heart of the Matter

Journal entry, May 11, 2007

The surprise visit could not have been more perfect. Got home at about eleven p.m. after winning two out of three in New York. We spent the day with a boat ride and barbecue after picking up Alexis from school and playing in the pool for about four hours. Alexis swims like a fish and Anthony is hilarious with the floaters on. He will be swimming in no time. He already grasps the concept of holding his breath.

Now into baseball. Almost a month since the last entry, and after reading it, almost all the sentiments are the same. Good situation, hitting for power, and doing a great job of driving in runs. Upright approach with hands close and very few strikeouts still. Believe seeing the ball well and still getting it done with two strikes as well.

We have a ridiculous $10\frac{1}{2}$-game lead in the division as we start a three-game set in New York. Everyone is doing their job and J.D. and Manny still have not gotten hot. Hopefully Josh's finger gets better once and for all, because we have had a great run of guys being healthy so far.

All is well and we need to keep it going, because it is fun watching the Yankees panic. Time to turn the knife because it is already halfway in.

By the way, it's a funny feeling that this is a .300-plus year. No letdown. Too strong mentally, and the plan and the hands are just too good.

*T*he Yankees taught me a lot. One of the lessons garnered from that organization was the importance of winning, and that's why even though New York came into our June 2 showdown at Fenway Park 12 games behind us in the loss column, I understood exactly how important every last pitch was when we played them.

During my years with the Yankees, I was also schooled in a certain way of playing the game, and I bought into it, hook, line, and sinker. So when the second day of the season's third month came around, and I found myself staring at the prospect of being tagged out for the front end of a sure four-three double play, it was time to show the teachers that the student hadn't forgotten.

I was standing at first base with the bases loaded in the fourth inning, and Jason Varitek hit a slow grounder to New York second baseman Robinson Cano. I found myself at a dead stop, with Robinson standing straight in front of me. Now, this was a big part of the game, with the bases full and us holding on to a 2–1 lead. If I tried to avoid him and simply went out of the base path, it was going to be an automatic double play. I was a dead duck—I realized that. But I knew if I could somehow prevent him from throwing out Tek at first, that would be golden. That's where the Yankee in me kicked in.

Coming up in the New York organization, we had a rule that you could never peel off between first and second when breaking up a double play. Even if it was a line drive to second base, and you froze, you had to run to second, and you had to slide. So sometimes guys would literally slide halfway in between the bases, which looked ridiculous, but peeling off was simply not an option. Another mandate was that if someone came at you while you were in the base path, he was open game and you should knock him on his butt, because then another runner might be able to advance.

Coincidentally, a few weeks earlier we were playing Toronto and a similar situation took place. Aaron Hill, the Blue Jays' second baseman, got the ball, and went to tag me, although he wasn't standing right in front of me. I was trying to race by him before he could secure the ball, but he got there first, causing nothing more than a little bump and an eventual double play. When we went back out to the field, I was talking with their third-base coach, Brian Butterfield, who spent many years in the Yankee organization as a coach. I talk to third-base coaches on occasion, such as Tampa Bay's Tom Foley (because he played with my former high school coach), but this conversation with Butter was more than just small talk.

"I told Aaron," said Butter, "that he had better just throw the ball to second, or just tag you with his arms extended, because you should lay him out." Butter hadn't forgotten the Yankee way, and, by the time Cano gave me another opportunity, neither had I.

At first I thought that maybe I could get in a rundown, allowing Tek to beat out the throw to first. But when I saw Robinson coming at me, I knew his intentions were to make a quick tag and throw to nail Tek. My choices had dwindled to one, so I lowered my shoulder, lifting Robinson off the ground and eventually putting him on his back. The hit looked nice, but the bottom line was that he got the throw off and completed the double play. Still, it was Red Sox–Yankees, and the night before that Kevin Youkilis had gotten into it with Scott Proctor after being hit in the head with a pitch, so this was another story line to feed baseball's most televised (and publicized) rivalry.

For me, it was a reminder that I hadn't forgotten how to play the game.

Tests like these had been coming my way for a good while now, and I had come to understand their worth. Maybe one of the first guys who really made it a point to force me to come up with the answers that mattered was a guy named Joe Arriola. Joe was a friend of my dad's who sponsored a lot of our summer-league teams, while also coaching our fall team at Christopher Columbus High School. This was a guy who made a fortune as the founder of Avanti Press, Inc., and became the city manager for the city of Miami, but still made it a priority

to coach us kids, even though his own son, an all-state wres-
tler, didn't even play baseball. He loved the game, and he loved
to test us.

The fall of my freshman year he invited me to practice
with the varsity, even though I hadn't made the freshman
team. There I was, five foot six, and a buck-thirty-five, trying
to keep up with a bunch of eighteen-year-old seniors. Joe was
going to hand me my first high school baseball exam, one that
he knew I most likely wasn't going to pass.

"What position do you want to play?" he asked. I told him
shortstop. It might have been a higher level, with greater dis-
tances between the bases, but I still felt comfortable in the
heart of the action. So Joe hit me a couple of ground balls. I
fielded them, and threw to first. No problem. But after the
third ground ball, he came over to me and said, "Mikey, how
old are you?" I told him I was fourteen. "Well," Joe continued,
"when do you turn fifteen?" I let him know my birthday was in
about three months, on February 24. "I know your father," he
said. "I want you to do me a favor. For your fifteenth birthday,
tell your father to buy you a new fucking arm, because you
can't reach first base."

At that moment I knew shortstop wasn't for me. I had officially been taught the importance of understanding both your
strengths and weaknesses when stepping on a baseball diamond, thanks to the eye-opening exam administered by Joe
Arriola.

It was on to second base, where I showed enough promise
to make the junior varsity team my freshman year, and be

integrated into the travel-team lifestyle the following summer. By the time my sophomore year came around, I had fallen in love with hitting, thanks in part to Joe. Understanding that I was willing to answer any examination thrown my way, he started opening more and more doors for me. During this period came the invitation to his batting cage, allowing for endless rounds of throws from the steel-armed pitching mechanism I became unbelievably familiar with.

Every afternoon I would head over with a buddy of mine, cranking up the mechanical arm faster and faster, while moving closer and closer. I would love to say that the endless afternoons of fine-tuning my swing were building my teenage work ethic, but the reality is that it's not work when you're having fun, and, for me, each day was three hours of fun. I simply loved swinging a baseball bat.

When practices in the fall began, I could tell that the hours of staring down the pitching machine had paid off. I was still only about 140 pounds, but I was keeping up with the bigger bodies. In our annual Blue-Gray Games, the intrasquad scrimmages to finish off the fall season, I went 8 for 11 and the coach singled me out in his postgame speech. That's what happens when expectations are low and results are high. My performance had set me up to make a run at varsity in the spring, even though second base was already occupied by Luis Hernandez, who was slated to play at the University of Miami the following year.

Throughout the fall season I was fortunate to witness Luis taking the same tack my father had all those years in youth baseball, helping out those who really needed to be helped. In this case, that was me. He taught me everything about playing middle infield, supplying a constant stream of instruction. "When you come to the bag here, make sure you do this so you can give this guy the feed; and when you throw to second, do this." And Luis was good, really good. So as much knowledge as he was dropping on me, I made sure there were just as many questions going back his way. I knew he was the one standing between me and varsity, but there was no resentment. I was just grateful for his help.

So with Luis at second base on varsity, I wound up on JV. But in retrospect, it was a pretty unique double-play combination we had: hitting eighth and playing shortstop, Alex Rodriguez; batting ninth and playing second base, Mike Lowell.

Alex was a long way from earning his current title as the world's most feared hitter. He was just a scrawny kid with a lot of talent. The JV team was our first time playing together, but we were later teammates in summer league. The player who had truly distinguished himself as the area's baseball star was another current major leaguer, Eli Marrero. Boy, he was the best. Eli was a year younger than I was, played catcher, and could run faster and hit the ball harder than anybody. Eli was at another level compared to us.

In the middle of that sophomore season, there was a moment when I believed I was primed to take a regular spot on varsity. Luis got hurt and couldn't play second base. But instead of promoting me, they sent up another kid who was also playing at second, and to make matters worse, he was a freshman. Not only had I been passed up to make the jump to varsity, but also I couldn't shake the thought that if they were putting this freshman in front of me now, how would I be able to crack the lineup next year? I was learning early on that very little in this existence as a baseball player was going to come easily. So I took a deep breath and told myself to wait and see what transpired in Legion baseball during the summer.

More bad news—they wanted to move me to third base. Making that throw, with less than 150 pounds behind me, wasn't happening. If I couldn't reach from shortstop, how was I going to make the toss from third? The bottom line was that while they called me a third baseman, the title was hollow. I wasn't in the plans for the Christopher Columbus baseball team.

Like a lot of kids faced with playing-time issues, I turned to my father for advice. The perception was that, since it was a private school, the more the parents contributed in terms of fund-raisers or concession stands, the more their kids had a shot at playing. Dad was involved with the team, but in his own way, which was, looking back, the right way. He had little patience for my accusations of favoritism. "If you don't have playing time, it's because you don't deserve the playing time."

Here I was, practicing with the varsity in both the fall seasons of my freshman and sophomore years, and now, when it was time to start getting ready for the big team in the summer leading to my junior season, I was on the bench. I was literally not playing. I was fifteen years old and miserable.

I decided I wanted to switch schools.

A lot of the guys I played with on my travel team, including Eli, were going to be at Coral Gables High School, and I lived in the Gables, so, technically, paperwork was all that stood in the way . . . paperwork and two parents.

To say Mom and Dad were hesitant would be an understatement. Gables is your regular public school, and the year before, a kid got shot there. They said it was nothing more than an accident, but that type of thing just didn't happen at private schools like Columbus. Ultimately, however, both my parents thankfully realized that my happiness was the most important thing. I was a good student, ranked third among three hundred students, and was probably going to get good grades no matter where I went. And, although he would never make a big production, my dad had also begun to change his mind and realize that the Columbus team was no longer the best situation for me. My mother was a tougher sell, agreeing to attend one of the games with my father to see what the problem was. Taking me away from the Catholic-influenced education wasn't the direction she had hoped for, although Mom was sympathetic enough to my plight to keep an open mind. After watching the two kids playing in front of me butcher some grounders, she turned to Dad on the way home and asked when the appointment for Coral Gables High was scheduled for. She was sold.

After one of the summer-league games, my father decided to approach the athletic director at Coral Gables to let him know of my intentions. They already knew me a little bit since the assistant coach of the travel team was a coach at Gables, which helped with the initial relationship. The process was in motion.

"I talked to the athletic director at Gables," Dad said. "All that he said was that you'll have a place. They will give you an opportunity to play, but if someone comes around and beats you out, and he's better than you, so be it. But I made sure that if you were good enough, you would get a chance to play." That was all I asked for.

After a couple of weeks, my dad took the next step, approaching the head coach at Columbus, Brother Herb Baker. "I just want to inform you that Mikey isn't going to be attending Columbus High next year." My dad told me later that he felt obligated to go to church earlier that morning because all he could envision was Brother Baker telling him that I wasn't good enough or something like that and Dad subsequently wanting to knock him out.

Luckily, that never happened. All Brother Baker asked was what school I was planning to go to. "He's going to Gables High," my dad responded. This wasn't foreign territory for the coach, considering that the year before three guys had left Columbus to play at Gables. And there would be one more notable transfer that summer, with Alex Rodriguez heading to Westminster because they said he wasn't going to play. So I don't know. You tell me. . . .

I did get to play varsity my junior year, starting at second base while hitting ninth. I finished with twenty-three hits, all singles and one double. Major-league aspirations weren't exactly boiling over at this point. I couldn't even get one single recruitment letter from a college, the kind that were flying around our team's mailboxes at every turn. I might have had one Division II school insinuate they would give me $2,000 in scholarship money if my parents were willing to pony up the remaining $17,000. I simply had no power at all. I could hit, but hitting .300 in high school is like finishing at .140 in the big leagues. I needed to grow, and luckily I did.

In the summer heading into my senior season, I began to finally put on some weight, with the scale now tipping at around 165–170 pounds. It was a big jump from where I had been the year before. By the time I joined up with an all-star travel team to play in Euclid, Ohio, momentum was on my side. Here I was playing shortstop against a team that included both Alex Rodriguez and the NFL quarterback Danny Kanell, and I was holding my own. I was in uncharted waters, but I felt confident. It was at that tournament, at the age of seventeen, that I hit a home run that actually cleared a fence. As I trotted around the bases, I came to the conclusion that it had been worth the wait.

Through all my struggles in high school on both the Columbus and Gables teams, I had faith that senior season was going to make up for it all. I was now six foot two, although at 175 pounds I was still fairly skinny. Less than three years earlier, I had been only five feet six and 140 pounds. But it was all coming together. We had a great group of guys, players I had grown up with in Little League and summer leagues. And best of all, we were kicking off the season in a tournament at

Columbus High. A pretty sweet reintroduction was in the works.

It didn't start as planned, with a 10–6 loss to Columbus in the first game of a round-robin tournament that included four teams. But we went on to beat our next two opponents, while Columbus did as well. So there we were, having to beat Columbus twice to win the championship, and third in the lineup was my name, still without a high school home run.

After Gables won the first meeting, fate reared its head in the title game. My first at-bat, boom! I hit a home run. Once again, the timing of the momentous event was truly worth the wait. And it only got better. My second at-bat, boom! Another home run. The game went back and forth, eventually leading to the point where I came in from second base to pitch, qualifying me for the win. And to add the proper punctuation to what would be our ticket to the championship, in my last at-bat with runners on second and third, Brother Herb Baker, the coach who almost ended my baseball dreams before they began, walked me intentionally. Him seeing me play was one thing, but having him actually fear my bat was about as sweet a redemption as I could have imagined.

That wouldn't be the last bit of revenge enacted that senior season, either. We would play Columbus again, this time in the regionals of the state tournament. I came in to pitch once again, with the game tied, and ultimately walked away with the victory. Nothing was said, but the scoreboard offered more than enough of a rebuttal. Later that year I would run into Brother Baker in the hallway at a high school sports award ceremony, where I was named one of the three finalists for student athlete and All–Dade County First Team. He said congratulations, nothing over-the-top yet hardly bitter, either. It didn't matter. I knew inside I had won the battle, and neither he nor I needed to say anything.

My instincts were correct that senior season. I did have a great year. I made All-Dade, and all-state, playing second base while picking up occasional pitching duties. (I finished the year at 9–0 but didn't save a game. I guess tied games were my forte.) The great thing was that I had become a legitimate Division I college recruit. Not bad for somebody who never hit a home run until his fourth year of high school.

The first university that wanted me was Florida International University, and they were relaying the message I thought I might never hear: "We're willing to give you a full scholarship." Other school offers were trickling in also. Notre Dame called me every Sunday—I guess like a good Catholic university should—talking to me for about half an hour each time. Pat Murphy, who went on to coach Dustin Pedroia at Arizona State, was an assistant at Notre Dame and was charged with getting the skinny second baseman from South Florida to come north. He was great to talk to, but no amount of charisma could make up for the fact that the Irish were offering only about $5,000 a year and my parents would be on the hook for another $30,000. That was a deal breaker.

The truth was, I had my heart set on one school, the University of Miami. I followed the Hurricanes religiously growing up, and went to the Ron Fraser Sports Camp there for four years in a row, having a blast every single time. And my brother, Carlos, was already enrolled. It all added up to my dream scenario. In my world, however, dreams hadn't been easily attained, and this one was no different. Miami did offer me a lot of academic scholarship money, but I wanted a baseball scholarship. The problem was that they were offering me just $3,000 a year, a number that didn't hold much chance of going up after they signed another local second baseman to learn under the tutelage of my old mentor, Luis Hernandez, who had been there for two years already.

FIU was going to be my next step.

When I arrived on campus, I was still reveling in the confidence gained from my senior season at Gables. My six-foot-three frame was still only about 180 pounds, but it didn't matter. I had a great freshman year. I ended up hitting around .370 and was named a freshman All-American. I was hitting the ball harder than I ever had in my life. Nothing, in my eyes, could stop me. Finally, I had put the pitfalls of the past behind me and could head into Waynesboro, Virginia, as the hotshot second baseman who was ready to tear up the Virginia Valley Summer League.

There were a couple of problems. First, the league used wooden bats. Second, my job for the summer was laying down sod at a local golf course. Spending the day hauling around pounds and pounds of turf before having to swing what seemed like a monstrosity of a hitting utensil was not ideal.

The Waynesboro Generals couldn't have been happy. I started the year 4 for 44, finally getting three hits the final day to finish with a .206 batting average. I was miserable. The bats felt so heavy, and if you didn't hit the ball smack on the sweet spot, it wasn't going anywhere. And just for the obligatory salt in the wound, my roommate, Juan "Chili" Munoz, who played with me at FIU, ended up winning the batting title. Every night, after the game, our host family would greet him with, "Chili, what a great game. Three hits." And then they would go over and console me, insisting the next day would be better. I was learning what it was like to struggle, and it was not a fun lesson.

When I got back to school, the self-doubt hadn't been left behind in Waynesboro. I was using aluminum bats once again, but it didn't matter. Questions regarding whether or not my freshman year had been a fluke started to creep in. The decision was made that I had to stop feeling bad for myself and start realizing my true lot in life. Those two months with a foreign hitting utensil weren't going to define me, but the two previous years would. The result of this self-searching was another great collegiate campaign, ultimately leading me to a hurdle I couldn't avoid, another wooden-bat league.

This time it was the Cape Cod League, perhaps the premier summer league for collegiate baseball players in the entire country. By now the sheepish feeling garnered in Virginia was long gone, and in its place was an entire new level of confidence, along with fifteen extra pounds of muscle. And it was the Chatham As who benefited. The wooden bat wasn't going to win this battle, with my average for the summer finishing off at .316, good enough to classify me as the top second baseman in the league.

I headed into my junior season at FIU once again swimming in positive vibes, some of which were gleaned from the fact that I could now hit the ball out of the park. In my freshman year I had hit three home runs, and six the next season, including three in one game. Now I was thinking that if I might be able to pop out ten or so in my junior year, and ride the momentum from my success in the Cape Cod League against some of the best college players, I would find myself in the top tier for the Major League Baseball amateur draft selection. There was one fly in the ointment, however. That junior season the school decided to build an entirely new baseball stadium, so we were forced to play at a park in Homestead. This place was wide-open, inviting wind to knock down each and every potential homer. It wasn't the welcoming mat I was looking for as I strove to become a potential draftee.

We had a good team, ranked eighth in the country for a time, and I had a solid year, but my total of only three home runs left me with a bit of uneasiness heading into draft day. Scouts from the Cleveland Indians were still coming up to me and saying that I would definitely go in the top nine rounds, which is all I really wanted, to go somewhere in the first ten rounds. These whispers helped a bit of the anxiety, but not much.

I had gone through the process to a much smaller extent in high school, having been drafted by the Chicago White Sox in the forty-eighth round after my senior year on the recommendation of an area scout named Pepe Ortega. Pepe called and told me the White Sox were willing to offer me $25,000 and pay for school, which for a guy taken in the forty-eighth round was a really good offer. Just being drafted sounded so cool. But I knew it wasn't an option in my house. This wasn't the road I was supposed to be taking. I was to go to school. My dad did say that if somebody offered me $200,000 to sign I should consider it, because you can always go back and get your education. But we knew that this "what if" was going to be a "never was," pretty much ending the drama before it got rolling.

If a player doesn't sign out of high school, he can't be drafted again until after his junior year of college, which was fine by me. This would give me an opportunity to construct a much more desirable package in the eyes of prospective employers, which, between the successes at FIU and the Cape, was a mission accomplished.

Draft day came, and so did hundreds of jump shots in my family's driveway as I waited for some sort of news. At this time there were no updates via cell phones or the Internet, so I was forced to resort to shooting the basketball while waiting for the phone to ring. That entire first day, it never did. Eighteen rounds of players were selected and I wasn't one of them. This wasn't part of the plan. Defiance immediately set in. I told myself that I was simply going to head back to FIU, get my degree, sign for $1,000, and love every minute of it. It wouldn't seem right if it came too easy.

The next day, early on, I finally got my call. It was from a

Yankees scout named Rudy Santin, whom I had met about five days earlier outside a local barbershop. He had asked me then, "If we draft you and offer about fifteen thousand dollars, would you sign?" I told him that they should draft me and then we could discuss it. I don't know if he could tell, but I simply wanted to be drafted, as early as possible, and get my professional life under way. Money wasn't weighing on me, but worrying about the impression left on teams was another matter.

The Yankees called and told me they had drafted me in the twentieth round. "Congratulations," they said. Great. Okay, so now what? I hadn't been drafted where I wanted, but I had been drafted. My happiness was tempered by my confusion over what had just happened, and what was looming in the coming days.

A few days after the draft, Rudy came over to our house and gave us the Yankees' offer: a signing bonus of $7,000. $7,000? That was it? There was a grant I could have received from Dade County for $2,500 per semester for people who got good enough grades and stayed at a Dade County–area college. So my thinking was that I was basically giving up money I could have had for school, which for me was money in the bank, for this $7,000. Are you kidding me? What happened to the mention of $15,000 outside the barbershop the other day?

My dad had done some research, and, thanks to one of his dental patients who was a scout, came across a printout of what twentieth-rounders had signed for in the past. "Look," I told Rudy, "I don't want to break the bank or anything. I just want to get what a regular twentieth-round draft pick gets." Then my father came in: "Okay, twenty thousand dollars and school, but I'm not going to negotiate. Twenty thousand dollars and school, that's it. That's twenty thousand dollars and two semesters of school."

Rudy came back with $12,000. Not good enough.

"No, I don't think you guys understand," my dad rebutted. "It's twenty thousand dollars and school, not nineteen thousand, nine hundred ninety-nine dollars. Twenty thousand dollars." This went back and forth for a few more days, leaving me with the uneasy feeling of desperation, to the point where I really didn't want to sign with these guys.

With the negativity still festering from all the negotiations, I went to lift weights for about two and a half hours with the catcher from my college team. This was the best therapy I could think of for the time being. But that night, a good chunk of the frustration was finally removed, as the Yankees called and told me they would pay the $20,000, but only one semester of school. "Nope," I said, "I need two semesters. I want to graduate." One semester at FIU cost $750. That was it. I couldn't fathom that the richest team in baseball was going to let me slip away for less than $1,000. I was right. They agreed to the terms, calling back and saying, "Okay, you're signed. But you have to be on a plane at six o'clock in the morning to go to Tampa tomorrow." As relieved as I was, I was instantly filled with thoughts of how sore I was going to be after lifting weights for the first time in four months, and how they would notice. I wanted to give off a solid first impression. What I soon discovered was that I should have been more worried about what they wanted from me.

"We want you to catch."

Upon arriving at the organization's minor-league complex across the state, I learned an eye-opening fact: The New York Yankees had drafted me in the twentieth round to become a catcher. I had barely ever caught, and really had no desire to catch.

"You're going to learn to catch bullpens and catch batting practice, and when we think you're game-ready, we'll put you there," they said. "But for the time being, the good thing is you're going to play every day at third base." Suddenly, third base, a position I had barely touched since attempting to get the entirety of my 140 pounds behind each throw in high school, didn't seem like such a parallel universe. At least compared to the thought of playing catcher.

I had caught a bit in Little League, which probably meant I had played more as a backstop than I had at third. I had played two innings at third base in a summer-league game, much to my dismay. The whole thing was surreal, but I was ready to try anything. Playing baseball as a profession was now my reality.

My first official professional baseball team would be located in Oneonta, New York, the site of the Yankees' New York–Penn League team. And it was there, in my very first game, that the business of baseball was about to slap me upside the head.

I looked at the lineup that day, the opener in a schedule that ran from late June to early September, and saw that I was hitting third. Our first-round pick, an outfielder named Shea Morenz, was hitting fourth. I couldn't help but be overcome with the irony. The guy slotted in the number-three hole had signed for $20,000, and had to haggle over $750 for school tuition, and the player right behind him was just given $650,000. And I suspect Shea wasn't being asked to learn the art of blocking wild pitches in his free time, either.

But the more I thought about the catching opportunity, the more I realized it might not be such a bad thing. Here I was, a guy coming off a college season with three home runs, clearly not the prototypical power numbers for third basemen. And, as a catcher, if you called a good game, which I thought I was very capable of, this might be a pretty quick ticket to the big leagues. But while I was slowly coming to grips with the idea of living the life of a catcher, the Yankees were in the midst of changing their minds. As the season in Oneonta unfolded, and I continued to wait for my call to don the catching gear, our manager, Rob Thompson, informed me that the organization had come to like the idea of my remaining at third base. Evidently, the fact that I had only one home run in the entire seventy-two-game season hadn't scared them off. They liked my hands, and knowing that I had at least finished with eighteen doubles offered some hope for me to grow into what most viewed as a power position.

We were all hoping that the strength would come, but there were no guarantees. By the time I began my second pro season, at Single-A Greensboro, I was getting stronger in small increments, still hovering around 185 pounds. One day our manager, Jimmy Johnson, was throwing batting practice for me, and when he finished he said, "Mike, I throw batting practice for you and I hear, 'Crack!' and I say that ball is gone. And then I look back and it only gets to the warning track. You remind me a lot of Ken Caminiti when I had him in the minor leagues. He had a good baseball sense, like you, but he was so behind physically. . . . That was all he lacked. You'll see. You're going to fill into your body, you're going to gain fifteen, twenty, twenty-five pounds in the next two years, and that's when you're going to be ready to play in the big leagues."

That was the first time anybody had told me I was destined to play in the major leagues. And knowing it was coming from a professional coach who had mentored a big leaguer like Caminiti just a few years earlier gave his words an added value. I hadn't made it yet, of course, but this was a pretty satisfying prediction, nonetheless.

After finishing my stint in Single-A, which was finished off with a twenty-four-game promotion at the next level on the Yankees' organizational food chain, Tampa, a decision was put in front of me. I had to go to Instructional League, leaving me with the possibility of not being able to finish my last semester of school. I was on the verge of starting the following season at Double-A if all went well in Instructional League, and that's just two steps from the ultimate goal, the majors. But this was my last semester, and I understood that with each passing year in pro ball it was going to be tougher and tougher to recommit to the classroom.

That's when my mom stepped to the plate for me.

"I'll go to class for you," she said. Mom had graduated with a finance degree twenty-five years earlier from the University of Puerto Rico, which just so happened to be the discipline I had also chosen. "I want you to graduate," she said. "You need to graduate now. You can't put this off any longer. I'll go to school for you for four weeks, if you promise, when you come back from Instructional League, that you're going to go to class." So, I promised, and my mom went to school for me. How unbelievable is that?

I was four classes shy, all of which didn't administer tests until the end. Mom would take three of these classes, with the fourth being held in a short span over the Christmas holidays. Four weeks she went to class, and four weeks she took notes. And when she was done, she gave all of the notebooks to me.

These were the most pristine, meticulous notes you ever saw. If the professor sneezed, she wrote in parentheses, "Professor sneezes." It wasn't going to be easy for me, because I would still have to digest a lot of information once the transfer had been made. But a deal was a deal, and I had made this deal with my parents upon signing on to be a professional baseball player. So when I returned from Instructional League, I limited my life to two things, going to the weight room in the morning and heading to the library in the afternoon. I had always reeled in As throughout my entire academic career, but this time around a C would have been acceptable. As it turned out, thanks to Mom's notes and my hard work, I got all As and Bs. I was going to graduate, and, to cap it all off, my experiences in Instructional League had really left an impression.

For the first time in my life I had taken up a regimented weight-training program, and the results were as awe-inspiring as Mom's knack for summarizing hour-long lectures.

When I showed up to spring training, I weighed 205 pounds. My six-foot-three frame had added 17 pounds since I had walked off the field for the last time the season before. Needless to say, it had been a productive off-season.

The diploma was nice, but the real payoff for my winter of activity came in my very first spring-training at-bat. First chance I got, I hit a home run to dead center field. Never, not once, had I hit a homer to straightaway center over a fence. The next day we headed over to St. Petersburg, where the Cardinals were training, and my first at-bat was off one of St. Louis's top prospects, Blake Stein. Pow! I did it again, sending the ball straight over the center-field wall.

Part of the explanation for my newfound power was the weights, for sure, but another part had to do with what I learned at Instructional League. It was there that I first met Gary Denbo, the coach who, eight years later, would help me rediscover my stroke. I was such a pull hitter, too much so. That had always been the case. So Gary and manager Jimmy Johnson got together and started flipping me balls, telling me to hit the same spot on the fence in front of me on each swing. The target was directly in front, right where the middle of the diamond would be. By the time I took this practice, and my newly discovered physique, into actual games, I was hitting so many balls up the middle and the other way that I became a little frightened that I had forgotten how to pull the ball. The truth was that I had become a more complete hitter, a better hitter, and a stronger hitter.

But I still didn't know where I was going to end up when the season started. About a week before the games were supposed to start, I saw the guy who had been playing third base in Tampa the year before still practicing with the Double-A team with me. I was a bit confused and concerned. I ended up asking the Double-A manager what the plan was. "I think you should have your bags ready to go up north," he said, insinuating that I would be starting at Double-A Norwich.

"Well, I have another question," I said.

"Are you going to get five hundred at-bats?" he responded, correctly anticipating my worries. "I envision you getting two hundred fifty to three hundred at-bats." That didn't sit well. I would rather start down at a lower level, get five hundred at-bats, put up some numbers, and keep on trucking toward the big leagues. The manager simply said, "Let's see how things play out." If the first game was any indication, it wasn't going to be worth the wait.

On opening day with Norwich, it was about eighteen degrees, the coldest game I had ever played in my life. In what turned out to be a thirteen-inning win, I was hitless in my first three at-bats. With runners on first and second, the same manager who had told me to let things play out was pinch-hitting for me with the other guy who played third and making it increasingly difficult for me to exhibit patience. I guess the good thing about these kinds of setbacks, and any other impediments that came my way, was that they offered a whole new flurry of motivation. And if there was one thing I knew how to harness by the time the opening-day substitution came around, it was the opportunity for some added inspiration.

I wasted no time, hitting .344 in 78 Double-A games. I had a goal to hit 12 home runs that year, and there I was with 15 by the time the All-Star break came around. That led to a promotion to Triple-A in Columbus, where, sure enough, in my first at-bat I hit a home run. There I was, one step away from calling Yankee Stadium my home, and I was not only playing—getting lots of at-bats—but playing at a level I hadn't experienced since legging out inside-the-park, Little League homers. I ended up hitting 15 more home runs in my 57 games with Columbus, while driving in 15 more during a playoff run that went to the limit of a championship series. I was keeping pace with the prizes of the Yankees farm system, while having undoubtedly punched a ticket to play in major-league camp the following spring training. The road had been paved and I found myself infused with positive energy.

I started the next year in Columbus, intent on keeping my run of good fortune on track. The homers and hits kept on coming, this time resulting in 26 long balls and a more-than-respectable .309 batting average. I was on the verge of the ultimate, and I knew it. A September call-up was going to happen and I was going to be a major-league baseball player. Jimmy Johnson was right. I did gain the weight and it was going to lead me to the majors. When he first uttered that prediction it was nice to hear, but it didn't mean the premonition was going to come true. But it did, and for all the right reasons.

I thought back to when it seemed like just one simple thing stood in the way of my big-league payday: finding some more muscle. As I hit the gym that off-season people there were talking about how prevalent steroids had become in baseball. I had been offered steroids myself, although it was always by strangers at various gyms, people saying things like, "I can get you what you want, clean." Clean? What's "clean" mean if it is on the streets? It wasn't for me, but I could definitely sympathize with those who succumbed to the temptation.

I saw it firsthand, the journeyman Triple-A guy who hits 12 home runs a year, is married with two kids, and is making $18,000 a year. All he needs is a little push and all of a sudden his salary goes well into six digits. For me, the transformation was simple genetics, my body filling into its six-foot-three frame. But for others, it wasn't that easy, unless steroids entered the picture.

As I would discover, steroids were a crutch. As time went on, the whispers got louder, and so did the denials. Me? I stayed out of it. I had put in a lot of hard work and dedication to put the pop in my bat, and now I was just focused on reaching my ultimate destination, the major leagues.

The door finally opened on September 13, 1998. I was the starting third baseman for a New York Yankees team that had already won 103 games. I was hitting sixth and ready to keel over from the excitement that came with performing in front of 47,471 fans at Yankee Stadium. And then in my very first major-league at-bat I singled up the middle off of the Toronto starter Kelvim Escobar. I had come a long way from a 145--pound second baseman who had had to switch schools just to hit ninth. Here I was with a hit in my very first trip to the plate in the big leagues.

I thought of my father and my father's journey and how I had gotten to this point. My fellow big leaguers had no idea what was running through my head, but I did, and that was all that mattered.

Statistically, my stay with the Yankees for the remainder of what would turn out to be a world-championship season wasn't all that special. I finished my 8 games with 4 hits, all singles. But what I did pick up during my time in that clubhouse was an excitement and sense of optimism about my future career. Being around guys like Paul O'Neill, Tino Martinez, Scott Brosius, and Bernie Williams instilled in me a whole new measure of professionalism. Not one guy on that team hit 30 home runs, but they knew how to play, and how to act. The result was 114 wins and the best club I have ever seen.

Toward the end of the regular season, I was starting to truly feel like I might belong, and, evidently, the Yankees were feeling the same way. New York's general manager, Brian Cashman, had approached one of my agents, Seth Levinson, and hinted at the fact that unless Brosius won the World Series MVP, which would put public pressure on the organization to re-sign him, the Yankees would be looking for me to be their everyday third baseman. The dream was just getting better and better. Here was a team that would have won the World Series in two of the last three years and I was going to be their third baseman?

But Brosius went out and hit .471 with 2 home runs in the Yankees' World Series sweep of the Padres, ultimately receiving a three-year extension. Even though Cashman had guaranteed Seth that my minor-league career would be a thing of the past, I was having my doubts. I shouldn't have. Cashman kept his word, putting me in the starting lineup . . . for the Florida Marlins.

On February 1, I got the word that I had been traded to my hometown team for three minor leaguers. It was amazing. Some misguided souls asked, "Aren't you upset you are being traded from the New York Yankees?" Are you kidding me? I was coming home with the chance to be an everyday major-league third baseman. They didn't understand that playing Triple-A for the Yankees, or any organization, is worse than the big leagues with the worst team in the world.

Sure, the Marlins were young, rebuilding and all of that stuff, but I could leave as many tickets as I wanted for all of my friends and family to see the end result of a story they had played a big part in authoring. Dad wants eight tickets? No problem. One of my buddies wants eight more? Sure. People point to the pressure that sometimes comes with playing in your hometown. But I didn't feel any of that. This was going to be fun.

Nineteen days later, that's when I found out about pressure.

CHAPTER FOUR

The Worst Nightmare

Journal entry, July 26, 2007

I have kept putting off writing and cannot believe how much time actually passes between entries. Well, I made my fourth All-Star Game, and although the travel to San Francisco was tough, and I didn't get much rest, I had a blast. We got good video and pictures, all of which will last a lifetime. The kids looked great with their Red Sox No. 25 "Lowell" jerseys.

Usually July is a slow month, but I've been hitting well and the RBIs keep coming. Hopefully I stay healthy because I really want to finish strong. We'll see later what the off-season brings baseball-wise, but right now things seem wide-open.

I have really enjoyed the summer with Bertica and the kids. They seem so happy to be with me and that makes me feel great. I am looking forward to a great off-season with hopefully a couple of getaways with Bertica and enjoying the kids, whether in the pool, on the boat, BBQing, or going to the park and riding a bike.

I feel like I have a good understanding of how to approach my off-season workouts and hope I can make some good gains.

Things are good and I even have a day off in Miami after the Tampa series. Four months down, two to go. Stay focused, work hard, and a strong finish is guaranteed. That's it for now.

N ot much had gone wrong in the 2007 season by the time August rolled around. We were still playing like the best team in baseball. I was locked in—keeping my same pregame tee routine throughout an entire season for the first time in my career, while earning a trip to my fourth All-Star Game—and most everybody's health remained in good shape. Even our biggest blow injury-wise, Curt Schilling's damaged pitching shoulder, appeared primed to right itself not too long after the July 31 trade deadline came and went.

And then there was Jon Lester.

Jon was a twenty-three-year-old pitcher who almost a year earlier had been diagnosed with a form of cancer, non-Hodgkin's lymphoma. After undergoing six chemotherapy treatments, and spending some time in the minor leagues, he made his return to a major-league pitching mound on July 23 in Cleveland. It was a big deal, and rightfully so.

I remembered when I heard about Jon's diagnosis, I was

surprised. They said he had lost twelve to fifteen pounds, prompting the tests that ultimately led to the identification of the disease. I didn't want to get in his way, or be another voice he felt obligated to listen to. All I told him was, "If you need to talk to me about anything, I'm here. Just handle your business. You don't have to please anyone. You don't have to talk to anyone, because you're getting calls left and right. Just get better and worry about baseball later."

I had known Jon for just a few months, but had been intimately familiar over the past seven years with what he was going through. He was joining a club to which none of us members wished we belonged.

I discovered my membership in the midst of the euphoria of my returning home to play for the Marlins. It was February 19, 1999, five days before my twenty-fifth birthday.

That was the day I went in to undergo my routine spring-training physical: eyes, ears, everything. It was supposed to be something as basic as going to brush your teeth. As always, the doctor told me to look to the side and cough while he examined my testicles. But then his face changed. He said he felt something a bit abnormal. The first question that came my way was if I had ever had an infection in the area, or if I remembered having any kind of collision. I didn't want to be sarcastic, but the reality was if I had experienced a significant injury in that area, I would have remembered it.

"Why don't you go to the bathroom and feel your left testicle, and tell me if you notice something?" the doctor told me. I followed orders, not feeling anything at first. But then I noticed a small bump. It didn't seem like much, but it was what had changed the doctor's demeanor, so it must have been something.

I had reached a level of physical fitness I previously didn't think was attainable, working religiously at the stadium with the Marlins' strength-and-conditioning staff, running sprints, everything. I was feeling stronger and healthier than ever. So I wasn't too worried when I followed the doctor's advice and headed over to the hospital for an ultrasound. But then after the procedure, I started to hear the people in the X-ray room whispering. . . .

"How about there?"

"Do you see there?"

"Yeah, I see that. We've got to tell the doctor."

What were these people saying, and why were they saying it? Did they think I couldn't hear them or something? I could see the pointing, the looks, the doctor coming in and nodding his head. Finally, the doc approached me and brought me into this circle of information.

"Mike," he said, exuding as little personality as possible, "when I read these things there are certain things, there are certain situations, where sometimes things arise. And in these situations, sometimes we have to take steps." He went on and on, rambling while beating around the bush and upping my frustration level to a new high. Finally, I had to step in.

"Doc, pretend you're talking to the wall," I said. "Can you tell me the best-case and worst-case scenario of what you're talking about?"

He told me the best-case scenario was that I would have to undergo surgery, but that I wouldn't need radiation or chemotherapy, and that maybe in a month to six weeks I'd be back on the field. That was the best-case scenario? There I was, trying to make this team, and I was going to miss all of spring training? For me that was a pretty bad best-case scenario.

"The worst-case scenario," he continued, "is you have surgery, they do the analysis, and it may be a progressed state of cancer." Whoa, cancer?! "Yes, cancer," he added. "You'll need radiation, chemotherapy, and then we'll see how far along it is. It might cost you about a year or so before we think you're healthy." And he wasn't even mentioning baseball.

Everything seemed so vague to me at the time. But that one word, "cancer," had hit pretty hard. It was a disease that had touched my family in the past.

My grandmother, Lydia Lowell, had passed away from extensive lymphoma on August 1, 1995, in the heart of my first pro season. I remembered just before I left for my dream job after signing, she was in the middle of chemotherapy and radiation treatments, having a catheter inserted into her skull so that the chemo could better reach her spinal cord. When I drove to my grandparents' house the night before leaving for pro ball, my father told me, "Make sure you give her a strong hug because you don't know if this will be your last."

As I said good-bye to my grandma, all she wanted to do was talk about me and my career. "Mikey, I know you will do really good things. You always seem to be on teams that accomplish great things, and oftentimes it's not expected.

Look at high school when you won the first title there in thirty years. And at FIU, you guys were ranked eighth nationally when no one thought you were that good." It was Grandma I pointed to in the sky when I won my first World Series, with the Marlins in 2003, because that victory was the epitome of what she had told me. Nobody thought we could do it.

And it was Grandma I thought of when "cancer" was thrown my way, the image of her during that final visit. Did I really have cancer? And would it be a death sentence?

The hospital was in Fort Lauderdale, north of Key Biscayne, where I was sharing a one-bedroom apartment with my wife. The entire forty-five-minute drive home, I cried. I couldn't tell my dad, and I couldn't call my wife. Here I was, married for four months, and I had to drop this on Bertica. I didn't know what to do. It honestly felt like a bad, scary dream, something I was going to wake up from the next day. I needed time to process all this information and put it in perspective.

But I understood I wasn't in totally uncharted territory, as two years earlier Bertica had gone through a scare of her own.

I met my wife at an end-of-the-year barbecue at Coral Gables High, where she was a sophomore and I was a junior. There were a bunch of us friends who went to the event, but one, Bertica, I really didn't know. I knew she was on the school's dance team, but I wasn't familiar with her name. I asked a girl I was friends with about her. "Oh, that's Bertica. She's great.

She's got such a good attitude, and she's always in a good mood." Eventually an introduction was made. But that was it. We all went to dinner at Denny's later that night. But no numbers were exchanged, nothing.

The summer of '91 came and went, and we didn't talk once. But the following school year, my senior year, I ran into Bertica in the hallway and "hellos" were exchanged. Amazingly, that was all it took. The road to a relationship was officially paved. In mid-November, we went on our official first date, to an amusement park–type place called Santa's Enchanted Forest. The night of skee ball and kiddie rides led to phone calls, and before long we were a couple. I went to college, and then the minors, but we remained together. We ended up dating for seven years before getting married, but I call them dog years because half of those years I never saw her.

My success never once factored into our staying together or Bertica's feelings toward me. She met me when I was the ninth hitter for a high school baseball team, without one dollar in scholarship offers. So either she was the greatest scout in the world or she truly did like me for who I was. I like to believe that it's the latter.

It was during one of those many times when we found ourselves apart during the seven years of courtship that Bertica received a horrible piece of news.

It was the summer of '97, I was in Triple-A, and we both knew we were going to get engaged in the off-season. What we hadn't planned for was what Bertica's doctors found in what was supposed to be a routine physical—a cyst on my soon-to-be fiancée's ovary.

The plan was for her to undergo surgery, have the ovary removed, and check to see if it could be something life-threatening. Looking back, I didn't grasp the severity of the situation at the time. But my parents, who had grown close to Bertica while we had been dating, tried to set me straight. "Say a prayer," my mom said, "because this is serious."

I was like, "We're just going in for surgery. They said she would be fine because, in the worst case, you can still have one ovary." I wasn't even thinking of the cancer thing because that dark prospect hadn't presented itself yet.

But I started to realize what a big deal it all was when Bertica called me before the surgery. "I think we should separate," she said. "I don't think we should see . . ." She didn't need to finish her sentence for me to immediately jump in and ask why. "What if we can't have kids?" my future wife responded. "I don't want to be the person that doesn't allow you to have kids."

That's when everything hit me. "No, no, no. We're a team here," I said. We were, and this team was going to come out on top. We did.

When Bertica underwent the surgery, I couldn't be by her side. I knew that ditching games to see my girlfriend in the hospital was going to be a tough sell to the organization. The reality of minor-league baseball this time wasn't sitting well with me. But the call from the hospital came, and it was good news. The cyst was benign, although they did have to remove the ovary. A bullet had been dodged.

About a month later I was reading a magazine article about the actor Pierce Brosnan. It went on to say how his life had changed after the death of his wife. She had had ovarian cancer. The story went on to describe how serious that kind of cancer was. My jaw dropped. This same malady could very well have taken the life of the woman I wanted to spend the rest of my days with. I immediately called my mother. "Mom," I said, "now I know why you were saying that." Here I was worried about getting hits in Triple-A, while my mother—a hospital social worker who has seen and heard all kinds of horrific things—was fearing for my girlfriend's life. Ignorance was bliss, but, after the surgery, all I could think about was how happy I was to be able to live my life with Bertica.

Yet, even with our previous experience with cancer scares, sitting down and telling my wife what the doctor had told me at that Fort Lauderdale hospital was one of the toughest conversations of my life. On my way home I had called her to tell her we had to talk once I saw her face-to-face. This wasn't something I was going to break over the phone. Bertica, who was working as a substitute teacher at the time, left school immediately and arrived back at the apartment shortly after I did. We both braced ourselves.

"They just told me I have cancer," I said.

Four months we had been married, and this was our introduction into wedded bliss. "I think I'm going to have surgery in a couple of days," I told her. "I've got to go back and do some more tests." Bertica was strong, having stared down her own traumatic episode two years before. "Well, let's just see what happens," she said. That was all we could do.

As we sat there in silence, I got a call from my buddies, who were supposed to meet me at the Marlins' FanFest, where I was scheduled to make an introduction on behalf of my new team. "Dude, you weren't at FanFest. What's going on?" one of them asked.

"Cancer," I told them. Then came a phone call to my parents. "Cancer," I uttered once more. Each time the word was met with utter disbelief. Saying it over and over didn't make it any easier for me to digest, either, but it did start to make it seem much more real. Repetition was driving it home. I hadn't been able to feel anything, and that's the thing that scared me the most. I hadn't been able to admit it. But after telling my wife, my mother, my father, my brothers, my sister, and my friends, I knew for sure. I had cancer.

The next day brought another trip to Fort Lauderdale, this time with the Marlins' team doctor, Dr. Kanell, who was the father of NFL quarterback Danny. There we met up with the specialist, a man named Dr. Paul Tocci. He was about to offer an introduction I never saw coming. "Congratulations," Dr. Tocci said. Here I was, having not slept all night, worried that death was right around the corner, and he was giving me kudos?

"If you're going to get any type of cancer, this is the one to get," he continued. "No matter how progressed it is, it's beatable." This was about as welcome an education as I had ever received. It wasn't guaranteeing recovery, or even survival, but at least it was offering hope. Two days later I was on an operating table.

I remember lying under the bright lights spread throughout the operating room at six o'clock in the morning. It was silent but everything about that morning was silent, the kind of silence when you're surrounded by friends and family who don't know what to say. In my mind, however, not a word needed to be spoken, because I understood that this wasn't a complicated matter. I needed to do this, because if I didn't I would die.

My only previous experience on an operating table was as a four-year-old, when I underwent minor surgery on the tubes in my ears. Unfortunately, a postoperative lollipop wasn't going to do the job this time around. The only way this was going to end well was for me to hear that the operation had given me a fighting chance to turn back cancer.

When I woke up, I had a feeling like somebody was stabbing a knife into my lower right side, just below my waist, especially when a cough came along. The pain was emanating from the area where they had made the incision to remove the cancerous testicle. Still partially drugged, I kept muttering about how I didn't understand why there was this pain in my waist. Surely, I thought at the time, the agony should be emanating from parts south of my belt line. I had no idea what was going on.

When they wheeled me into my room, the support system was already there, all my relatives, along with a few friends.

But the face I immediately locked in on for some reason was my grandfather, my mother's father, whom I had become extremely close to. His name was Eugenio Lopez-Ona and he was the one who had taught me how to play tennis, how to play golf. He was the kind of guy who never really showed emotion—and here he was crying. Seeing my *dad* cry in that room wasn't all that shocking, considering he would weep upon getting a Christmas present. But my grandfather—that was an awakening. It made me think, *Wow, this must be really serious. If he's crying, this must be* really *serious.*

The physical pain was one thing, and it lingered in my stomach for days to come. But what was even harder to deal with was the confusion I felt about how to move on with my life.

My mother was especially helpful in this regard. She was always great at confronting adversity head-on and figuring out how to put things in perspective and move forward. Of course, this was what she did every day in her career as a social worker. And she saw that the quicker her patients could get back into their everyday lives after a trauma, the quicker was their road to recovery. Now I was Mom's client.

"All right, let's go. It's time to go home," Mom said. "We're going to take you home now." I was in a state of befuddlement, partly because I was still under the influence of a healthy dose of prescription medicine. Why was my mother telling me to suck it up and get out of a hospital bed when my scar was still throbbing with pain? I just stared at her, waiting for her to come to her senses. She let it go.

But five or ten minutes later, she was at it again. "You look a lot better," Mom exclaimed. "Let's go. C'mon, we're ready." It was clear that my mother wanted me out of the hospital. But we couldn't just leave without the doctor's permission. The doctor had said he'd release me if, and only if, I was able go to the bathroom. That was it. "But I have no desire to go to the bathroom," I told the nurse, knowing full well that pushing out urine would be about as torturous an act as I could imagine. "Well, here's a big jug of water, and if you can't go to the bathroom in about twenty minutes, we're going to put a catheter in you," the nurse quickly explained.

"What's a catheter?" I asked. An answer was given and suddenly I knew what I had to do.

"Okay, don't worry. I'm going to go to the bathroom," I said firmly. And for the next fifteen minutes, I drank more water than I had ever drunk before. My hope was that by putting too much liquid in my system there would be some kind of overflow, and I wouldn't have to push it out of me. I wasn't sure if this strategy was sound, but I knew I needed a plan, so that was it. Anything was better than a catheter.

After twenty minutes the nurse came back in and asked me how things were progressing. "Man, I really feel like I have to go to the bathroom," I said. What a lie that was, but I was willing to say anything at that point. I ended up squeezing out a few drops of urine, which was enough to satisfy my caretakers and get me a pass out of the hospital. So I got in a wheelchair, left the doctors and nurses behind, and made the painful transition back into our one-bedroom apartment. Having to endure the agony that came with simply climbing in and out of bed soon made me second-guess my dumb bathroom plot. But I knew Mom was right. It was time to get the healing process going. And I was about to receive some very good news that would accelerate that process.

The cancer had been caught at the least progressive stage, meaning no chemotherapy. But I did have to go through four weeks of radiation. I wasn't out of the woods, but a path had been cleared. A happy ending was at least in sight, but the road to get there wasn't just going to be lined with get-well cards and balloon bouquets.

The first step was making a trip to, of all places, the sperm bank. Although my baby-making equipment would be protected from harmful rays during the radiation treatment by a metal plate, that didn't mean precautions shouldn't be taken. Bertica and I wanted a family, and even though she now had one ovary and I had one testicle (we often joke we're a perfect fit), if there was an opportunity to bring kids into our life, then we were going to do whatever it took to make sure we got there. So, a week before radiation began, the first deposit was made.

When I went through that first round of radiation on the Monday after the surgery, it didn't seem like that big a deal initially. I was lying there, and then, ninety seconds later, I was done. That was it. Sure, they told me I was going to start feeling tired, but that didn't seem too daunting. But two hours later I found out just how frightening this stretch was going to be. I started throwing up—I mean nonstop yakking. It got so bad that by the time I finished my flurry of vomiting—a run of about eight different meet-and-greets with the toilet—I had absolutely nothing left in my system. And when I did try to replenish with some sort of food, it didn't stay down for long.

The next day, it was the same routine: prep for the radiation, spend ninety seconds under the beam of light, and then go home for another round of projectile puking. This was hell. I couldn't see myself lasting for four weeks of this. By the end I would probably have lost fifty pounds. *There must be another solution,* I thought. And there was, though it was an expensive one. The doctor told me there was a medicine called Zofran that would help ease my radiation-induced pain. The problem, he said, was that it cost about $2,500 for a four-week dose. "No problem," I said. "I've got Major League Baseball insurance. Are you kidding me? Of course they'll cover it." They didn't. But I didn't care. I would pay any amount of money to remove this evil from my body. Zofran to the rescue! From that second day of radiation on, I never threw up again, although my stomach did feel irritable all the time. No matter. It was better than the violent vomiting.

After two weeks I went to see another specialist, who told me things were progressing rather well. He even gave me the option of upping my dosage, which would allow me to complete the entire radiation nightmare a week early. It seemed like a superb alternative. I couldn't imagine feeling any worse than I had over the last fourteen days. Although I wasn't throwing up anymore, I was completely wiped out, like all the life had been sucked out of me. I had no strength to do

anything. One day I tried to go out onto my high school baseball field in Coral Gables, but I only took ten ground balls and
then succumbed to exhaustion and couldn't go on.

Throughout the entire recovery process, my family was
my rock. My two brothers were great, ready to do whatever
was needed to help. But it was my sister, Ceci, who showed me
how to find my courage.

Seven years earlier, just a week or so after Hurricane An-
drew had turned the South Florida community inside out,
Ceci was hanging out in a friend's backyard, and they started
playing with a chain that had been left on the ground. They
were whipping the chain around, and it ended up striking my
sister in her right eye, scratching her eyeball. She was whisked
to the Bascom Palmer Eye Institute, and the doctors didn't like
what they saw.

Ceci had to undergo surgery. But after she did, things only
got worse when an infection was discovered in her retina. It
was bad. The doctors told her she had to spend the next two
weeks lying facedown on a table—not unlike a massage table,
with a doughnutlike ring for her to see through. We bought
her a small television to watch through the doughnut hole, but
we all just felt so bad for her.

Here was this little ten-year-old girl, my sweet baby sister,
thrown this awful physical ailment, which ultimately took away
her sight in one eye. It was horrible. But what really made a mark
on me was how she bounced back. Within a week or so after her
treatment ended, she was back at school and getting straight
As. And it wasn't long before Ceci was back in the stands, next

to my dad, at virtually all of my college games, meticulously keeping score. It was a beautiful image, and one that I never forgot as I trudged through my own recovery.

And just in case I ever started to forget, I had a permanent reminder in the form of a little rock Ceci had given me during my treatments with the word "Trust" written on it. And on the other side was the inscription: "As long as you trust in what you're capable of doing, you're going to be able to do it." That rock stayed with me. In fact, to this day, it sits on my desk so I can look at it all the time.

Ceci and I will always have a special bond because we both were struck with something early in life that most people don't experience in an entire lifetime. Her resiliency helped me find my strength, and I knew that if my ten-year-old sister could overcome everything she had, then so could I.

And I did.

When my three weeks of agonizing pain came to an end, I was ready to jump back into baseball. So, the Friday after my final treatment, I dove into a car and drove to Melbourne, with my parents following close behind. It had been almost exactly a month since I made that tear-filled trip home from the hospital, worrying about how I was going to tell my wife and family about the cancer. But this time my car trip north to the Marlins' baseball fields was filled with nothing but smiles. Even though my body had not recovered, I felt invigorated. Nothing, not even cancer, was going to stop me from getting to the major leagues.

But when I got there I started to feel a bit nervous. Normally, I would be feeling nervous about whether or not I was ready to play baseball at the highest level. But today it was more that I was overwhelmed by the new environment. This was a new team and a new collection of teammates, most of whom I had never met before. I felt like a kid on his first day of school. And to make things worse, all eyes were on me because of the media attention surrounding my cancer.

Everyone had their questions. "How do you feel? How do you feel?"

"I feel great," I said. I was lying. But how do you stand up there and justify being back on the baseball field by telling the truth, which was that I felt like crap? I knew I would get back to normal sooner or later. Right then, however, it just wasn't sooner.

The next day I was told I would be building back up to my old self with the Triple-A team. The plan was for me to lead off every inning for six at-bats. I was still weak, but putting a baseball uniform back on gave me a shot of adrenaline and I went 4 for 6 with two doubles and a home run. Not bad for my first time up against a live pitcher in nearly six months. The next day didn't disappoint, either, with two more hits. I decided I was officially ready to be the starting third baseman with the Marlins, and others seemed to think so, too.

But then I was brought back down to earth by Rick Ankiel, one of baseball's top pitching prospects at the time, who supplied me with seven hitless at-bats. Ouch. He was a good pitcher, but it was also that I wasn't ready. I had dropped my bat size from thirty-two ounces to thirty-one, and it still felt like I was swinging a tree trunk. I just couldn't do it. Something as simple as a round of ground balls left me utterly fatigued. It all added up to my beginning the season with Triple-A Calgary. It was unavoidable, and, actually, not all that bad. Because Major League Baseball had given me permission to take as long as I wanted on what was considered a rehabilitation assignment, they allowed me to still make major-league money. The paycheck was unbelievable. I made more money in that month and a half than I had in my entire previous three and a half years in the minor leagues.

As the first month of the season came and went, my strength crept back, and the tendonitis that lingered in my throwing arm became a thing of the past. Finally, our manager, Lynn Jones, told me that the Marlins' general manager, Dave Dombrowski, wanted to talk. Dave, who has always been good to me, said, "Look, Kevin Orie strained a quad, and he's going to be put on the disabled list, but it's retroactive for four days. So that means he's got eleven days. I'm hesitating to call you up because after these eleven days, if I send you down, you don't have the rehab anymore and you'll be back to making Triple-A money. What do you want to do?"

"Are you basically telling me I have an eleven-day trial?" I asked. Dombrowski told me that was, indeed, the case. "I'll take those chances," was my response. Are you kidding me? All I wanted was to be in the major leagues.

At the time I was batting .300, but with absolutely no power, none at all. There was very little authority behind any of my hits, resulting in just two home runs and three doubles in twenty-four games. I was reverting to the powerless stroke I thought I had left behind in the minors. Jones said, "Look, I'm going to tell Dave what I think. I think you struggled with guys that throw with above-average velocity, and you're really struggling with off-speed stuff." He wasn't cutting me much slack, even though I hadn't seen a pitch for six months after coming off of cancer treatments.

So with these doubts firmly planted in the general manager's head, my eleven-game tryout began on May 29, which was the same day as my older brother, Carlos's, birthday. I took that as a sign that it was going to be a good day. No luck. No hits in four at-bats with two strikeouts, and a throwing error. And the next day, when the first at-bat resulted in a strikeout, I found myself with five at-bats with my new team, three of which had resulted in strikeouts and one in a double play. Not good.

But on my second at-bat of the day, I hit a rope off of the Cincinnati starting pitcher Steve Parris into the left-center-field gap. As I started breaking out in a sprint toward first, my eyes were on their center fielder, Mike Cameron, who was running this glorious line drive down. He was running, running, running, and then finally it went over his head. Okay, it was just a simple double, but, believe me, few hits in my career have offered such a sense of relief. I was back in it. All that cancer, radiation, weakness was behind me now.

Another sacrifice fly in my next at-bat, and a single against reliever Danny Graves in the eighth had put me on the track that some thought I'd never see after exiting Calgary. And better yet, I managed to keep up the momentum right up until Orie returned, which meant I got to stay in the majors while other members of the Marlins made various trips to the DL. I wasn't playing every day in the major leagues, but I was finally a full-fledged major-league player.

I still remember the day when I finally realized I had reached that next level, after a year of exhaustion and rust. It was a game in Arizona on September 18, and it was the instant I became a starter in the major leagues, for good.

I wasn't even supposed to be playing that game. The Arizona ace Randy Johnson was on the mound, I was hitting only about .250, and we had already lost 90 games. So I was pretty sure I was out. And I took the opportunity to grab some gym time. I hit the weights, hard. How was I supposed to know Orie was going to hurt his wrist during batting practice? But he did, and with only fifteen minutes until the first pitch. So, with my arms still burning from my curls and crunches, I got the word that I was in the lineup against one of the most feared pitchers in the game.

I started out pretty much as I expected to, going hitless in my first two at-bats. But then, third time up, I got a 3–1 fastball from Johnson and launched a two-run homer well over the left-center-field fence. Hitting home runs is nice, but doing it against a talent like Randy Johnson adds a little extra something. The next time up I was facing Gregg Olson, and along came another hit, this time a soft single. Then came the punctuation. In the ninth inning, with the Diamondbacks carrying a two-run lead, I turned on a 97-mile-per-hour fastball from

My father, seen
here pitching for St. Joseph's
University, experienced his fair share of great
moments on the baseball field, ultimately leading him to
induction into the Puerto Rico Athletic Hall of Fame.

Courtesy of the Lowell Family

Not too many nine-year-olds
get a chance to represent
their country, but that was
the case when I went to
Japan to play in a baseball
tournament. The trip was
a tough sell for Mom, but
after Dad relayed his own
experiences on travel teams
in Cuba, I got the go-ahead.
I'm on the left in the photo.

Courtesy of the Lowell Family

Thanks in large part to Dad, things worked out pretty well by the time my senior season at Coral Gables High School came around.

Courtesy of the Lowell Family

From my senior prom at Coral Gables High in 1992, with the woman I would one day make my wife.

Courtesy of the Lowell Family

Both my father and I couldn't help but smile after I signed a letter of intent to play at Florida International University. For a kid who had one extra-base hit his junior year of high school, getting a chance to play for a Division 1 school showed just how far I had come. Courtesy of the Lowell Family

The beginning of our relationship with my agents, Sam (*second from right*) and Seth Levinson (*second from left*). I don't know if they knew what they were getting into that day, but their guidance has been invaluable throughout my journey. Courtesy of the Lowell Family

One of the best moments of my life
November 7, 1998, our wedding day
Courtesy of the Lowell Family

Getting a chance to haul in a big one with Marlins teammate Jeff Conine after hauling in the bigges
one, the 2003 World Series title. The whole experience in '03 wouldn't have been the same withou
the club to which both Jeff and I belonged, "Two Sticks." Missing from the photo are fellow "Tw
Stick" compatriots Mike Redmond, Brian Banks, and Andy Fox.
Courtesy of the Lowell Fami

I have never seen anybody come through in the clutch time and time again better than David Ortiz.
Courtesy of the Boston Herald

This fifth inning double against Colorado in Game 2 of the World Series gave us a 2–1 lead, which would stand until Jonathan Papelbon nailed it down in the ninth. It was probably my biggest postseason hit in the 2007 playoffs.
Courtesy of the Boston Herald

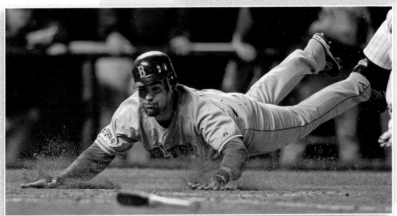

My beating the throw home on Jason Varitek's fifth inning single in the fourth game of the World Series gave us a 2–0 lead and allowed for one of my most memorable dashes to the plate.
Courtesy of the Boston Herald

Being awarded the trophy for
Most Valuable Player of the
2007 World Series.
Courtesy of the *Boston Herald*

Celebrating Alexis's fourth birthday with my father-in-law, Jose Lopez. I will always value the sacrifices Jose made, spending fifteen years in a Cuban jail as a political prisoner.

Courtesy of the Lowell Family

...w many kids get a chance to use Fenway Park as their playground? I am enormously grateful I have ...ten the chance to watch Anthony and Alexis grow up in Boston.

Courtesy of the Lowell Family

For me, it doesn't get much better than getting a chance to celebrate a World Series championship with my son, Anthony, along for the ride. Courtesy of the Lowell Family

My biggest fans, my family: (*from right to left*) Dad; Mom; my older brother, Carlos; my sister, Ce Victor, my younger brother; and the guy who got them all of that Red Sox gear.

Courtesy of the Lowell Fan

Matt Mantei, sending it over the left-field wall to hand us the lead for good. It also had the effect of putting me in the starting lineup indefinitely.

By season's end I had hit .253 with 12 home runs in 97 games, which, considering all that had transpired, seemed reasonable. As the final games trickled off the schedule, Dave Dombrowski told the players he was going to hold individual meetings to let everybody know exactly where they stood. Mine came with about a week to go in the season. Dave said nothing more than, "You're going to be our starting third baseman and you're going to hit fifth. Do you have any questions?" I told him, "No."

Dave went on to ask me if I wanted to know about any of the other positions on the team, and again I answered, "No." And that was that. I was now officially a starting third baseman entering a major-league season.

It was a gratifying way to end what had been an unbelievably challenging few months. Surviving cancer was, and will always be, my toughest battle. I laugh when people talk about how tough it is to deal with the boos of fans or the high expectations of big-market baseball. Hah! You want to know what tough is. John Kruk knows. Andres Galarraga knows. And Jon Lester has come to find out. When cancer comes calling, baseball takes a backseat. Having forty thousand people at Yankee Stadium tell me I suck is a nice diversion.

But it wasn't just the cancer that made 1999 such a tough year for me. While most people knew about my cancer, radiation, and subsequent comeback, they didn't know about another big challenge that came up during my rookie season. It was something that truly opened my eyes up to the darker side of my glamorous new life as a big leaguer.

In July of '99, I was still in the midst of my comeback from cancer, and Bertica was heading to the beach with one of her best friends (we will call her "Pam"). As they were driving across a bridge, adjacent to the Port of Miami, they were both admiring the sight of the cruise ships docked nearby when Bertica, who was driving, took her eyes off the road and found herself too close to the median. It gave her a sudden fright and she overcompensated, sending the car swerving across three lanes and smashing into the barricade that prevents cars from plunging into the water. The automobile was wrecked, air bags had been deployed, and Bertica's friend was hurt. It was an ugly situation.

I was on my way to what was then known as Pro Player Stadium, our home park, when I got the call. "Mike," Bertica said, "I've been in a huge accident." She said she was fine, but Pam had been taken to the hospital. Later, I found out that my wife's friend was banged up pretty badly, and had been unconscious. After more than twenty-four hours, she finally regained consciousness, thank God. And after a few days had passed, she started to talk. Her first words: "I want everyone out. Only Bertica is able to stay." They had been close friends, and now they had been through this terrible accident together—so it made sense that she wanted to talk to Bertica alone.

We had only one car at the time, so we got in the habit of

me dropping Bertica off in the morning at the hospital to visit Pam and then picking my wife up there after my games. Bertica would have gone to the hospital to visit regardless—this was her best friend—but of course there was also the sense of guilt my wife felt because she had been the one driving the car. It wasn't easy on either of them.

After a couple of weeks, Pam was released from the hospital and the doctor said she was going to be fine. We went over to dinner at Pam's house and she seemed to appreciate Bertica's friendship. But just as things were starting to get back to normal, Pam stopped talking to Bertica. She wouldn't return any of my wife's calls. Bertica tried writing a letter but no response. We phoned mutual friends to find out what was going on, but no one seemed to know the answer. Then we finally got our message.

A letter arrived stating that Pam was suing us for $1.2 million. My jaw dropped.

Here we were, in the first year of my major-league career with less than $8,000 in the bank, and somebody was trying to take some of my potential earning power over the next four or five years.

I knew this wouldn't be happening if I was still in the minors. Because I was a big leaguer, there was now a target on my back, and it was in the shape of a dollar sign.

The case ended up going to mediation—an option usually executed so as to not flood the court system and to instead find a quicker resolution. So Pam's lawyer started telling us all of this stuff about Pam's blurry vision, headaches, and more.

And how it should be a $2 million lawsuit, but because of his client's friendship with Bertica it was only $1.2 million. "One point two million?" I protested. "Are you kidding me? I've got eight thousand dollars in the bank!"

At that point, a family friend of ours who was an attorney gave us a good piece of advice. He understood what kind of dent this was going to put in the life Bertica and I were attempting to build. He told me I had to bring my W-2 tax forms to the mediation session so that they could see that $1.2 million was not even a possibility. So I brought the documents, going all the way back to when I signed in 1995. The papers showed that in those first three months of my first pro season I made only $2,800. The following year I made $9,000, in '97 it was $13,100, and in '98 it went up to $37,000, but only because I got called up for twenty-something days and made $1,000 a day in the majors.

Everybody on Pam's side of the table looked like they had just seen a ghost. They honestly believed everyone in baseball had $5 million at their fingertips.

I gave them a moment to digest the new info. Then I said that if they wanted to sue me for something, they should look at the last four years, during which I hadn't even made $60,000. That's when they walked out of the room and talked again. It was determined that a settlement would have to wait.

So that was that for the time being. I went through my first full year in the big leagues and ended up having a pretty good season, hitting 22 home runs, driving in 91 runs, and proving that I was, indeed, an everyday player. When the season was over, Dave Dombrowski called the Levinsons. He wanted an extension, which was going to end up totaling $6.5 million. I had entered a whole new salary level. But Seth was hesitant, concerned that the deal would open the door for Pam to come back after us with the lawsuit. "I'm not giving up six point five million dollars because of one point two million," was my response.

But more than any concerns regarding the money was how the whole saga had affected my wife. Her spirit was crushed for about two years. I mean, this had been her best friend ever since she was fifteen. And over all the years, the bond between them had never wavered. I was mad because I felt that Pam's demands were driven by our perceived financial situation. But my wife was mad because she believed that her best friend had turned on her for nothing more than money.

I ended up signing the deal for my extension, and when it became official, Bertica asked, "Is that good money?" I told her that if nothing else it represented an opportunity to not worry about the lawsuit anymore. We ended up getting a letter saying they were cutting their demand in half, to $600,000, and after another mediation, we ended up settling for more than $300,000. It had been three years since the accident, and two years since the first mediation, but at least now it was done. Pam had reentered society and was holding down a steady job. Needless to say, writing that check for $300,000 was not one of my happiest moments. But it was worth it to put the past behind us.

I definitely don't want to downplay the fact that Pam was

in an accident and did get hurt. It was a very serious thing; it could have taken her life. But I know that if I was in a car crash with one of my best friends, it wouldn't even cross my mind to enter into a lawsuit. That's what I just couldn't understand.

It took Bertica a long time to open back up to her friends, or find new confidantes, and put them at the same level of trust she had formed with Pam. Time heals many of life's scars, but it was only natural that she continued to keep her guard up.

Despite everything that happened to us in '99, I still came away with the foundation for a major-league career, and, most important, I had my health. The lawsuit was a big, expensive ordeal, but my recovery from cancer sure put things in perspective.

Every six weeks I returned to the Sylvester Cancer Center for blood work, X-rays, and checkups, and every time I walked in the door with my fingers crossed. "Please don't come back," I would whisper in my head. "Please nothing come back. Please nothing come back." Then, after a year of the process, I had to head in to the center every three months. I did that for the next two years. They told me that if the cancer hadn't returned after two years, the chance of it coming back was less than 5 percent. That was my first sigh of relief. Then came the five-year mark, where they say that if you clear that, the odds of it returning are the same as the odds of contracting it in the first place. So on the day of my five-year mark, February 19, 2004, we had a full-fledged celebration at the Lowell house.

In fact, to this day, we continue to celebrate every February 19. Sadly, this date had already held a spot in my psyche even before the anniversary of my diagnosis—it was the birth-day of one of my buddies, Peter Carbonell, who was killed in a car accident when we were attending grade school. So it shouldn't be too difficult to understand why I was so happy to be able to finally associate February 19 with something good.

Now, on February 19 I think about how I made it. But there was a time during my march to that five-year mark when it appeared as though I might fall a year short.

The way 2003 began, it looked like it was going to be the greatest time of my life. I was another step closer to turning back cancer for a fifth straight year, and I was hitting the ball like never before. In the first month I totaled eight home runs. In May it was eight more, and then I hit nine for June. It was an incredible feeling. Here I was, in the third week of June, and I already had my career high in homers. Every single ball I hit hard was finding its way over the fence. It was unbelievable.

Now, it was this kind of power potential that made people whisper about the possible use of steroids when that power disappeared two years later. But the reality was that I never took steroids, although at one time I thought I might be forced to. After my cancer surgery I asked the doctors with the Mar-lins if I needed testosterone supplements because my body was supplying less testosterone now that I had only one testi-cle. I was sure that if my body needed it, Major League Base-ball would give clearance. And if that was the case, and my own well-being was at stake, I wasn't going to turn away from a solution.

But the doctors told me that it was actually just the opposite, that my body would adjust—and if I did take testosterone, or anything related to steroids, it would raise my testosterone levels to a point where my healthy testicle was going to be fooled into shutting down. That's where any talk of supplements ceased for me. But, when the home runs started coming in bunches, and then they took a hiatus, the facts didn't stop some from making accusations behind my back. That I resented. The success I embraced.

But I didn't get to sit back and enjoy that success for very long before more bad news came my way. It had been only a month since I had received the happy diagnosis of fibrous dysplasia—not cancer. "Fibrous dysplasia" have become my family's two favorite words. The nightmare was over and the rest of '03 was shaping up to be more like a fairy tale. No such luck.

In the eighth inning of our game against the Montreal Expos at what was now called Dolphin Stadium, I stepped to the plate against the relief pitcher Hector Almonte. We were in second place with 72 wins, unexpectedly contemplating life after the regular season, and I was at a previously inconceivable 32 home runs. Then came Almonte's 3–0 fastball.

The ball was coming right at my head, so I put up my hands in self-defense. The pitch hit my left hand flush on the back side, taking my legs out from under me, lifting me into the air and onto the ground. I can still hear the sound it made, like a gunshot, followed by the astonished drone coming from the stands. There are some times when you get hurt, and there is an instant flash of pain but you know it's not going to turn into a more serious injury. That wasn't the case this time. I didn't have a good feeling about this one, and when the trainer came out to remove my batting glove, the feeling grew even worse. I knew this was more than a bruise.

They took me back into the trainers' room, ran some X-rays, looked at them, and took all of twenty seconds to give me the news: "You have a fracture." It was plain as day. My only hope was that it was one of those microfractures that would only keep me out a couple of days. Again, no such luck. "No," the doctor said, "this is going to be four to six weeks." I was devastated.

Derrek Lee, our first baseman, came in and asked, "What do we got?" I broke the news to him that it was broken. "Damn!" he said. That's when a sense of guilt set in. It was two days before the waiver trade deadline, and I was putting my team in a real bind. The Marlins' front office immediately tried to smooth over the situation, trading for Jeff Conine the next day, allowing him to play in the outfield, with our twenty-year-old phenom, Miguel Cabrera, sliding into my spot at third. We went 18 and 8 in the final month, and made the playoffs, so my guilt was tempered.

Four weeks after I was struck by Almonte's fastball, I went back to the hand specialist. The entire month was a race against time, considering I had to show the Marlins I was able to hit if they were going to put me on the playoff roster. Now I was going to find out if the bone stimulator that had been attached to my hand for the last few weeks had done its job. All

I wanted was clearance and then, pain or no pain, I would show them I was fit to swing a bat in the postseason.

The specialist took my hand and started poking and prodding, pressing and pulling. It hurt, so much so that I couldn't hide the pain.

"I don't think I can clear you for at least another week," he said. That, I told him, was unacceptable. He couldn't understand why I was so impatient. I tried to explain that even if the Marlins made the playoffs that week, they would still want me to show I could swing a bat before putting me on the playoff roster. And if I wasn't activated for the first series, they weren't going to let me come back on the roster in the middle of the action without having shown that I could contribute.

"Look, let's do this," he said, seemingly sympathizing with my plight. "You can do tee work today and we'll see what happens." Fair enough. Then came another crimp in my plan.

As I was driving home from the doctor's office, I got a phone call from a person who will remain anonymous—but he is someone who was privy to the inner workings of the team's decision makers. "What did the doc tell you?" he asked. So I filled him in about how the doctor had eventually given me permission to hit off the tee. "Just do me a favor," the voice on the other end of the line said. "You do everything in your power to be able to hit this week." The insinuation was that the Marlins had already locked in their lineup for the playoffs, with Conine in left, Juan Encarnacion in right field, and Cabrera remaining at third. "It didn't come from me," he said, subsequently hanging up the phone.

Here I was in the middle of a career year, and the organization was making me feel like I had no chance of coming back. Their cleanup hitter was on the edge of returning and they were shooing him away. Needless to say, after the phone call, I was filled with rage. So I called my dad to vent, and then he passed the phone to Mom. That's when I received a shock. My mother, usually the cautious one, asked, "What's the worst that could happen, you break your hand again? Well, then you've got six extra weeks to heal in the off-season. So you might as well go as hard as you can." For Mom, this advice was highly out of character.

I decided to go to the cage to do some light tee work with a few soft tosses. My hand was killing me. You know how a little kid gets when he is trying not to cry to show he is really a big boy? That was me—it was so hard not to break down and submit to the pain. All the trainers were there, as was our manager, Jack McKeon, and our hitting coach, Bill Robinson. Bill asked me, "How does it feel?" It was a question I knew was coming, but I was still hoping to avoid it.

"Man, it feels really good," I said, just dying inside.

When we were done training, everybody went their separate ways, with Jack and the trainers going to their respective offices. I headed for the clubhouse attendants' room, which was just a little back office out of the way of the usual comings and goings of the team. As soon as I entered the office, I just broke down, finally succumbing to the pain that had tested my restraint for the last hour. I looked up and saw that the clubhouse attendant was watching me.

I called my dad once again, this time letting out the tears as I spoke. "Dad, I did it!" I told him, trying to control my sobbing. "It killed me, but I did it."

My father's advice was to wait and see how I felt tomorrow. He understood my dilemma: the time constraints I was under, having to first show the Marlins I could hit at all, then take batting practice, and finally produce in a real game. All of this with just five games left in the regular season. The next day I did show up for another round of tee work, except this time I made sure to pop four Advils before picking up a bat. It felt a little better, so I played it cool. I told the trainers that I might want to ice a little after the session, but in reality I yearned to plunge my hand into the cold stuff for at least the next three hours.

But the next day I felt even better. And then, with the wild card already wrapped up, I got my chance. It was all I needed. The result was nothing more than a simple broken-bat soft liner over the third baseman, highlighting my three at-bats for the day. But that was enough. Two days later I discovered that all the teeth grinding and hidden tears had paid off. I was on the playoff roster.

The pain was behind me and I couldn't imagine something like that ever happening again. But four years later, in August '07, I got hit hard again in the same way on the back of my hand.

It was right around the same time of the '07 season as my incident in '03. The Tampa Bay pitcher Andy Sonnanstine was on the mound, and another fastball was bearing down on my head. And, sure enough, once again I put up that left hand out of instinct, trying to somehow protect my face, or anything around it, from the 86-mile-per-hour offering. But this time I had protection.

In '03, after I was hit by the Almonte pitch, Jeff Bagwell, the longtime Houston Astros first baseman, sent me one of the pads he had used for some time on the back of his batting glove. But while the thought was in the right place, this wasn't for me. It just didn't feel right. That didn't mean, however, that I wasn't wary about being hit again. So I kept looking for an answer, and finally found one thanks to the Red Sox rehabilitation coordinator Scott Waugh.

Early in the '07 season, after I was hit by a pitch from the Yankee starter Chien-Ming Wang, Waugh offered to affix a pad—something made of the same hard plastic as a catcher's knee pads—to the back of my batting glove with some Velcro. That little piece of plastic probably saved my season. When the Sonnanstine pitch in August '07 ricocheted off the pad, the sound was eerily similar to the moment in '03. But the feeling, thankfully, wasn't the same. I bent over in obvious pain, but this time I could move my fingers and hand. I was fine. It could have been ugly, really ugly, but, thanks to Waugh and, in an odd sense, Hector Almonte, the errant pitch was a relatively harmless twist in my journey.

Pitches that zone in on my head haven't always been a bad thing. One time in '06, a fastball off the noggin actually helped cement my relationship with a Red Sox fandom I hadn't quite gotten to know yet at the time.

We were playing at Fenway Park and Adam Loewen, a big lefty for the Orioles, was throwing, and throwing hard. There are certain times during the year at Fenway when the days are getting a little longer, and the light can get tricky. This time, the view of Loewen's release point was definitely going to be difficult as we got through the early innings, which was a bit unsettling, considering this guy was throwing 94 miles per hour. Hitting that kind of velocity is tough enough, but to do it while having to guess where it's coming from, now that's a challenge. Loewen had already gotten two strikes on me, so I was just looking to protect the plate, when at the last second I saw the ball coming right at my head. This time my hand wasn't quick enough.

The ball hit me flush on the helmet, jettisoning the protective gear clear off my head and sending me to the dirt. Immediately the checklist began: I was conscious, check; I could think straight, check. *Okay,* I thought, *this looked a lot worse than it was.* Believe me, when a major-league player gets hit in the head with a major-league fastball, that isn't always the case, helmet or no.

The trainers and Terry Francona came flying in, but I immediately assured them: "No, no, I'm okay." But they didn't want to take any chances, and they ordered me to stay still. I couldn't comprehend why, thinking they knew something I didn't, like I was going to start fainting in ten minutes. Tito then chimed in, "How many fingers do I have up?" raising two digits. "Seven." He looked back at me with a serious expression. "I'm fine, Frank." I always love messing with Tito, and this was another great opportunity to do just that.

Two innings after I toyed with Tito, I saw Baltimore's Nick Markakis loft a foul ball over toward the stands along the third-base side. By this time, I had stopped thinking about the fastball to my head from earlier in the game. Other than a slight bump, I was fine. So I went all out and chased Markakis's ball over to the railing, where there was a little bit of padding at knee level. Believe me, you're always a little bit braver when padding is involved. As it turned out, I judged the distance wrong, thinking I had one more step than I really did. The result was me flipping my body into the crowd, although my glove stayed up because I had to brace my body with my other arm. Fortunately for me, this time the ball found the proper landing spot, my Wilson A2000. It looked good and we got the out. In the eyes of the fans, that's all that mattered.

The next time I came to the plate, everyone in the stadium rose to their feet. They had loved my play, all the more because it had come after my getting hit in the head earlier in the game. What an amazing gesture. I was overcome with gratitude, but I didn't know what my proper reaction should be. A tip of the hat would have to suffice. This I did know—the moment was a turning point in my relationship with my new home city. It didn't take a rocket scientist to understand that if you played hard and the right way, it wouldn't be difficult to get along with Red Sox fans.

That standing ovation, along with the RBI single and steal of third that followed, made it an extraordinary day. And on top of all that, it was the day I got introduced to what would become one of my favorite rock songs. My next at-bat after the show of appreciation from the fans, the Fenway sound system blasted the Black Sabbath classic "Iron Man." I had no idea of the significance of the title or the words until after the game, when some guys came up to me and were like, "Man, Black Sabbath. I like it. That's a great song." I responded sheepishly, saying, "Yeah, Ozzy Osbourne . . . of course." I had had no clue about that song before I strode to the plate that day. But after seeing the fans' reaction, and my hit that followed imme-diately after the first chorus, I was sold. For a year and a half, Ozzy and I have been inseparable.

CHAPTER FIVE

The Playoff
Payoff

Journal entry, October 17, 2007

Well, I will start this one off by saying we've dug ourselves a hell of a hole. Down 3 games to 1 to Cleveland in the American League Championship Series and having to face C. C. Sabathia tomorrow. Maybe this off day takes all the good karma out of their clubhouse and into ours. I really think if we get back to Boston we can take them. Game by game, don't look ahead.

Let's recap the postseason. We swept Anaheim but things weren't that easy. David and Manny are crushing the ball and we won a huge game two with a three-run walk-off by Manny. I think it was the farthest ball I had ever seen hit at Fenway. Game three was close but we blew them out late. Schill was pinpoint. What an ability to execute location! Even more impressive was how he's had to change from straight power pitcher to more finesse.

Speaking of power pitchers, Josh has been lights-out. I know he had huge expectations put on him b/c of how he pitched in the '03 playoffs, how his season unfolded, and all the hype in Boston that comes with being a No. 1 starter. Not sure these expectations are fair, but he's going above and beyond. It seems like his concentration goes to another level in the playoffs. Would go to war with him anytime. Hopefully tomorrow he extends the season.

Been swinging well in the postseason and driving in runs. No need to stop now. Was a great feeling to get a curtain call after my game two homer. Nothing like these fans.

I know this is a lot of baseball and no family, but considering where we are, I'll catch up later. LIFE IS STILL GOOD!!

*W*hen I think of the playoffs, I think of all the lessons I learned from Mike Redmond, the Minnesota backup catcher and one of my best friends in the game.

I remember first seeing Mike when we were both with the Marlins, and immediately thinking, *Man, this guy had better really call a good game, because he doesn't do anything. He isn't in the greatest shape, and he doesn't have much power at all.* It didn't take long to find out where Mike's value rested. During my rookie year one of our pitchers, Alex Fernandez, said that there were two catchers he considered the best in terms of throwing to, Mike LaValliere and Mike Redmond. I still had doubts, asking Alex what made "Red" so good. "Dude, he's so on top of the game," Fernandez said. "I never shake him off. I'll go five innings at a whack without shaking him off once." For a major-league pitcher like Alex, it was rare to have so much faith in a catcher. I soon found that Mike was, indeed, one of a kind.

It was Red I thought of when we fell behind 3 games to 1 in the best-of-seven American League Championship Series against the Indians. We, the '07 Red Sox, were a good team that had done a lot, winning the organization's first American League East title since 1995, and conducting a neat three-game sweep of the Angels in the divisional series. But now we found ourselves one game away from negating all the promise we had shown over the last nine months, one loss away from going home.

For me and Josh Beckett, at least, this wasn't new territory. Back in our run toward a World Series title in '03, our Marlins team had been in an identical 3-games-to-1 hole to the Chicago Cubs. It was Red who seemed to carry us out of the abyss then, so I was going to try to do the same.

Red didn't play much that year, an understandable situation considering he suited up behind perennial All-Star backstop Ivan "Pudge" Rodriguez. But playing time, or a lack thereof, didn't prevent Mike, or any of the other Florida bench players, from making their mark.

The perfect example of Red's influence came in the middle of a losing streak during the '03 season. We were in Cincinnati, where the batting cage is connected to the clubhouse. All of a sudden Mike marched into hitting coach Bill Robinson's office wearing nothing but high-top spikes and batting gloves, saying he was ready to do his hitting drills. Here he was, bad body and all, looking for any way possible to snap our losing skid. So Red went out, hit buck-naked, and we proceed to win. He did it again the next two days, and each time we won again.

Now we were back in Florida, where there is a huge window to the batting cage so that everybody in the public concourse can see. That wasn't going to stop Red. Once again, he came out with his spikes and batting glove, this time carrying a bedsheet to prevent the public from looking in. When it was all said and done, there were five straight naked Mike Redmond hitting sessions, and five straight Florida Marlins victories.

It was a great group, particularly the collection that included Red, Brian Banks, Andy Fox, and Jeff Conine. These guys and I called ourselves "Two Sticks" (named after what it looks like when someone gives you the middle finger with both hands). Every morning at eleven o'clock on road games we would get together for breakfast. If you were five minutes late, you bought that meal. And then after the game the get-together was over beers in the hotel lobby. Banks would drink ginger ale, for which we'd tease him mercilessly. But it was all in good fun. That's just how it was with the Two Sticks. We all loved to play baseball, talk baseball, and give one another a healthy ration of shit. That's what made it all work.

And when we found ourselves facing the end of our season against the Cubs, we were all in it together—all of the guys from Two Sticks, along with a collection of truly dependable bench players, such as Lenny Harris and Mike Mordecai. Every three outs, whether we gave up runs or not, we'd all be yelling, "All right, guys, let's go, let's go. That's a good job. We'll get it back."

Late in the season Red began an anthem. Every time we

would come back into the dugout, he'd start shouting, "Push, push, push. Grind, grind, grind." Then he went, "Push, push. Grind, grind. Push. Grind. Push. Grind." At first this nonsensical chanting was somewhat annoying. Some of us jokingly fired back, "Shut the fuck up, Red!" But then one inning he went silent, and all hell broke loose. "Hey, Red, what happened to, 'Push, push, push. Grind, grind, grind'?" And a few wins later, nobody cared about how grating it was. We wanted him to say it every single inning. It worked then, so I thought maybe three years later, with an entirely new team, it could do the trick once again.

I believed in the power of "Push, push, push. Grind, grind, grind. Push, push. Grind, grind. Push. Grind. Push. Grind." Now it was my job to show my new teammates the light. So every time we came in to hit, the words were repeated. Over, and over, and over, starting at the commencement of our comeback, and lasting the entire way through. This time I also added another element, chopping our hitting coach, Dave Magadan, in the ribs after each recital.

"What are you doing?" Mags asked upon first being introduced to my ritual.

"I don't know, but it might work because it worked about four years ago," I said. That was all the explanation needed. From then on, starting in game five in Cleveland, through to the final out in Colorado, the words never died. As soon as my foot hit the top step of the dugout after each third out, the guys started in. "All right, we've got to push. We've got to grind!"

I knew the chant had entered the fabric of our team's existence before game two of the World Series. We have a little bulletin board in the training room as you head upstairs to where we eat. People usually post funny things on the board, stuff from the Internet and good-natured ribbing. Everyone reads it and nobody is spared. But this time the words of the day were "Push, push. Grind, grind." I took my camera phone, snapped a picture, and immediately sent it to Red. He deserved to see it.

The '03 Marlins and '07 Red Sox were distinctively different teams, but I had found a common thread.

Finding your team down 3 games to 1 in a best-of-seven league championship series is not a great feeling, but the presence of Josh Beckett on the mound offers about as much peace of mind as can be mustered in such a circumstance. I first discovered this about Josh in '03 when we, the Marlins, were presented an elimination game against the Chicago Cubs, with one of their aces, Carlos Zambrano, charged with closing it out for the Cubbies. But, thanks in large part to Josh, there was at least a semblance of optimism regarding a potential comeback. In some ways we had no choice but to believe. All we had to do was look at our luggage. Upon showing up at Dolphin Stadium, our bags were packed not only for two games in Chicago, but the first pair of World Series games in New York that might subsequently follow.

Josh didn't disappoint, giving up just two hits over all nine innings while striking out eleven. It was one of the best performances by a pitcher I had ever witnessed. The 4–0 win gave us the chance to take advantage of our packing expertise, and it allowed me something more. With my two-run homer in the fifth inning—a shot that gave us a lead we wouldn't relinquish—it cemented my residence in the starting lineup. Things had been uncertain after my hurried comeback from the broken hand, so the playoffs seemed to me like another reward for perseverance.

Before I hit the game-five homer, I had been trying to prove my worth to our manager, Jack McKeon, since the first game of the series. In the divisional series against San Francisco, I didn't make an appearance in either of the first two games, but I did start game three, which I viewed as an extremely classy move by McKeon. He didn't need to start me, with Jeff Conine, Miguel Cabrera, and Juan Encarnacion all playing well, but he did. Unfortunately, there would be no reward for McKeon's decision, with his new starting third baseman going a weak 0 for 3. I had no chance. The media came up to me and pumped me for my thoughts on not playing in the first two games. I answered as honestly, and innocuously, as possible, saying, "I just want to win," which I did. But the fact was that I really wasn't all that upset I wasn't playing because I felt like I really couldn't succeed in my current state. I didn't want to play if I was not going to play well.

The adrenaline that had helped convince the Marlins to put me on the playoff roster had officially worn off, leaving me overmatched in the Giants series. And it didn't help that I had hardly seen any live pitching in more than a month.

But four days later, at Wrigley Field for the National League Championship Series, something clicked. In the time we had while waiting for that game one, I took a round of batting practice that gave me hope. I could suddenly grip the bat with an ease not felt for some time. I found ten straight swings where reverberation wasn't a factor. I took five good ones. Stopped. Five more. Stopped again. That was it. I didn't want to push my luck.

The next day I knew I wasn't playing, but I did take another round of batting practice. The newly discovered comfort level was still there. For the first time since being hit in the hand by Hector Almonte's fastball in late August, I knew for sure I could contribute. But it still took eleven innings and the use of virtually every other player on the Marlins' bench for McKeon to discover what I already realized.

With the score tied 8–8 and Chicago reliever Mark Guthrie on the mound, Jack sent me up to lead off the inning. He had little choice. The relief pitcher Ugueth Urbina was due up next, and our primary pinch hitter, Todd Hollandsworth, had already been used. On the sixth pitch of the at-bat I got into one, sending Guthrie's pitch over the center-field fence for what would be the game-winning run. Somebody was smiling down on me, because the way I looked, and felt, less than a week before, such a feat would never have been an option.

The moment also led to the greatest voice mail message I have ever heard.

Kevin Millar, a former teammate of mine in Florida, was in New York with his new team, the Red Sox. He was in town to play the Yankees in the American League Championship Series, and he had gone to a sports bar with my agents, Sam and Seth Levinson, to watch our game against the Cubs.

As my at-bat against Guthrie was unfolding, Millar was on the phone, giving me play-by-play via a phone message.

"Your forearms look small," he said as the first pitch came and went. "Your eyebrows look too big," was the comment after the second pitch. Then, after I fouled a pitch off on 3 and 1, Millar goes, "Here comes the pitch. Let's see what you can do. . . ."

All of sudden there was an explosion of shouting into the phone. I had hit the home run, setting Millar off into a fit of yelling and running through the sports bar. "You did it! You did it! You Cuban! You did it for Elian." The fact that he was referencing well-documented Cuban refugee Elián González at this time of jubilation just added to the surreal nature of Millar's rant. In my mind it was the best voice mail ever.

By game three, with the series back in Florida, I finally got another start, claiming one hit. I was in the lineup again the next game, that time suffering through 0 for 4. So despite the euphoria I had soaked in from the first game of the series, there we were, down 3 games to 1, and I was sitting at 2 for 12. The good news for the team as we walked into game five was that Josh was pitching, and everybody had made sure they had packed enough underwear for an extended playoff run. The bad news for me was that, in my mind, getting my name on the lineup card seemed an impossibility. But desperate times call for desperate measures, and I guess McKeon thought I fit that bill perfectly.

My first at-bat I rifled a single to right field. And then came the chance in the fifth, when Zambrano threw me a cut fastball, which I absolutely crushed. It was a feeling that had eluded me for months but had now appeared at the most opportune of moments—the feeling that all I had to do was hit the ball, put my head down, and jog around the bases, because I knew that park had no hope of keeping the baseball in play. There I was, having gotten two huge hits in the playoffs, and what kept reverberating in my mind was the doctor's recommendation that I sit out the postseason in order to heal my hand. I think I can safely say that there was no better medicine for what ailed me than those two playoff home runs.

But by the time the eighth inning of game six arrived, unfortunately it was starting to feel like the doctor was going to get his wish. With Mark Prior and the Cubs cruising to a 3–0 lead with one out in the eighth, our off-season was just five outs away. We were even hearing whispers in our dugout that the Cubs had begun to prepare their clubhouse for the traditional champagne-soaked celebration.

But then Mark Redman became a prophet.

After a Juan Pierre double (just our third hit of the game), our second baseman, Luis Castillo, lofted a lazy foul ball along the stands adjacent to left field. As the ball drifted toward the stands, the Chicago outfielder Moises Alou gave chase. But just as Alou reached up, a man sitting in aisle 4, row 8, seat 113 by the name of Steve Bartman reached up and snagged the ball before it could ever meet up with Alou's glove for a potential second out. As Alou slammed his glove down, yelling in the direction of Bartman, our scheduled starter for game seven, Redman, was also bellowing to whoever in the Marlins dugout would listen: "Let's make him famous. Let's make him famous." In other words, let's make this live on in history as the time when a fan cost the Cubs a game.

Redman shouted those words over and over, until we finally did make Bartman famous (or infamous) in the eyes of Cubs' fans. Castillo ended up walking, Ivan Rodriguez came through with an RBI single, Miguel Cabrera's grounder was bobbled by Chicago shortstop Alex Gonzalez to score another run, and then Derrek Lee, a player who had been unfairly criticized for not coming up clutch, ripped a two-run double to left. Suddenly we were ahead, Prior was out of the game, and stadium security was forming a protective shield for Bartman. We scored four more runs, won 8–3, and headed to the hotel not only with a feeling of invincibility, but actually believing that the curse people say has been preventing the Cubs from winning all these years might not be that far-fetched.

Something else that didn't escape our attention during that comeback was the magic touch of our manager. We didn't see it at first. Leading off that eighth against Prior, McKeon chose to let the slick-fielding yet light-hitting Mike Mordecai take his turn at bat. Whispers immediately went up and down the dugout questioning the matchup, and, sure enough, Mike flied out. With five outs between us and the end of our season, the perception of wasting an out didn't go over well.

But after our Bartman-induced roll, giving us a 4–3 lead, Mordecai's spot in the order came up again. This time, facing the reliever Kyle Farnsworth, Mike ripped a double into the left-center-field gap, scoring three runs and basically guaranteeing at least one more game.

While Bartman's gaffe, Redman's proclamation, and Mordecai's second chance will forever live in my memory when I think about game six, I will always remember the next night by a much more conventional happening—another mind-bending performance from Beckett.

The game started with Miguel Cabrera hitting a three-run home run in the first off of Chicago starter Kerry Wood. But, two innings later, Wood exacted his own justice by launching a game-tying two-run blast to knot things at 3–3. I remember saying, to nobody in particular, "Are you telling me we're going to lose game seven because a pitcher hit a home run off of us? This is unbelievable!" In the third the Cubs took the lead on another two-run home run, this one from Alou, driving our starter, Redman, from the game. Our feeling of invincibility earned from the night before was slowly evaporating.

It was after those home runs, by Wood and Alou, that I came to realize how loud Wrigley Field could get. Up until game seven of the American League Championship Series against Cleveland in '07, when Fenway Park took the postseason decibel level to new heights, I hadn't heard a noisier venue. It wasn't just the people in the stands, either. There were twenty-five thousand fans in the streets outside the stadium getting their voices heard inside the confines of Wrigley, as well.

But, that night, no amount of noise could ruffle the kind of magic Beckett was bringing.

Josh was unstoppable. Three nights earlier he had thrown 115 pitches over nine innings. And now, with us hanging on to a two-run lead, he was coming in to pitch four more innings. Make that *dominate* four more innings. Even during the game, we were marveling at what he was doing. Some guys go out and don't pitch very well, and then they make excuses like, "Well, hey, I was on two days' or three days' rest." We knew that Josh would never use such alibis. We also had a pretty good idea he wouldn't need them either. The truth is that if it wasn't for Josh's performance that night, we wouldn't have gotten the 9–6 win, and we wouldn't have gotten a shot at the Yankees in the World Series.

The chance to play in the World Series was undeniably amazing, especially considering all that I had gone through to get to that point. But I would be lying if I said it wasn't at least a spot more meaningful because it was the Yankees we were going against. Did I want to show the team that traded me it had made a mistake and was paying for it in the form of a World Series title? Absolutely. Of course, those words weren't going to come out of my mouth while the series was unfolding.

As far as the media knew, facing the Yankees wasn't that big a deal to me. I made it clear that I had only been with the

New York big-league team for one spring training and one month in '98. It wasn't like I was with these guys three, four, or five years. That was my company line. The games were intense enough, so the fire didn't need to be fueled.

We walked into Yankee Stadium for that first game like we had nothing to lose. One would think that we were pretty cavalier for a team in the World Series, especially a team as young as we were. But that's *why* we seemed carefree; we were young and simply didn't know any better. We had no idea what kind of intensity or focus we were supposed to display before these games, so we simply made up our own pregame routine and watched the movie *Slapshot*. In our mind that was the approach we took to get to this point, so why change? We weren't going to let the surroundings dictate our behavior. As Josh Beckett said at the time, "We just might be stupid enough to win this thing."

The first sign that this tactic might actually work was in the very first at-bat of the series. We had been drilled by the advance scouts that nobody had gotten a bunt base hit off game-one starter David Wells all season. He was a lefty who was surprisingly nimble for his size. So what did our leadoff hitter, Juan Pierre, do on the second pitch of the game? He bunted for a single.

And before we knew it, we found ourselves in the sixth game of the World Series, at Yankee Stadium, with an actual chance to win the thing. And if that didn't make us giddy, the sight of our starting pitcher that night, Josh Beckett, sure did.

After the first four games, I was just 2 for 17, although

Jack was still hanging with me, keeping me in the starting lineup throughout. In game five I finally rewarded his faith, notching a two-run single into center field to extend our lead to 6–1 after five innings. And by the time we left Dolphin Stadium that night with what turned out to be a 6–4 win, I was starting to bask in the emotion of the moment. With Josh on the mound, and our team one win away from a championship, I could actually soon be celebrating a World Series victory on the Yankee Stadium field—against an organization that didn't think I could hit with enough power or could field my position well enough to break into its lineup.

I thought about how far I had come since battling cancer four years earlier, or since the time later on when I thought I was going to have to fight off the disease again—and even since recently when I worried that the broken bones in my hand weren't going to heal in time for the playoffs.

It isn't hard to recall most everything about that night: fifty-six degrees, packed house, and a perfect view of one of the most dominating clutch performances I had ever witnessed. From where I was standing, it was clear that Josh was more than up to the task. All it took was watching him pitch to Derek Jeter in the Yankees' first at-bat. Three pitches, three strikes, one strikeout. And it only got better.

By the middle innings Josh was not only cruising through the Yankee batting order—they never did get a runner to third base—but he was doing it using all of his pitches. There was no doubt Beckett's high-90s fastball was his most identifiable weapon, but his curve had suddenly made a strong appearance.

I became aware of this after watching the Yankee outfielder Hideki Matsui, who rarely allows a breaking pitch to fool him, display one of those check swings that identify a hitter's indecisiveness. As someone who has been there, I knew it is a bad feeling getting caught in between, and it must have been even more agonizing for Matsui, considering he almost never found himself in such a predicament. As soon as I saw Josh's pitch to Matsui, I instantly thought, *Oh, my God, this guy's stuff is unbelievable!*

And when the Yankees did hit the ball hard against Josh, it was inconsequential. In the eighth inning, for instance, Alfonso Soriano led off with a single. At that point it was a 2–0 game, and I knew that despite Josh's dominance so far, the good times could change with one swing of the bat. But that wasn't happening, not on that night. After a fly out, Nick Johnson hit a rocket right at our second baseman, Luis Castillo, who gobbled it up and tossed to shortstop Alex Gonzalez, who finished off the inning-ending double play with a throw to our first baseman, Derrek Lee. Three outs away. And those three outs came quickly enough—eight pitches from Josh, to be exact.

The first thing that struck me as we woke up from our dream to realize the 2003 Florida Marlins were world champions was how deathly quiet Yankee Stadium had become. The last out was made, a dribbler down the first-base line by Jorge Posada that Josh fittingly fielded himself, and the place instantly went silent. What you could hear was our screaming friends and family, who were sitting about twenty-five rows up into the stands but had now commandeered the stadium. The only regret regarding the postgame celebration was that we couldn't truly get to one another in what is a fairly tiny visitors' clubhouse because of the oppressive media presence. Still, that wasn't going to stop the boys from Two Sticks.

With champagne being tossed about, and at least ten members of the media hovering around each player, the members of our club, Two Sticks, gathered up the World Series trophy, a few cigars, and escaped to the field. Mike Redmond, Brian Banks, Andy Fox, Jeff Conine, and I ventured over to the spot behind home plate where the World Series logo was painted, placed the trophy in front of us, threw up our middle fingers, and took the picture we would treasure forever. Later that night, four shots and a glass of ginger ale (for Banks) closed the club.

Four years after experiencing the pendulum that was the playoffs, I was at it again, this time with a Red Sox team that was anything but young and naive to the world of postseason baseball. We were the big, bad favorites, going up against a Cleveland team whose construction throughout the previous few years had led to this moment. But while our payroll might have suggested an edge over the Indians in the way of top-to-bottom talent, it wasn't translating. After three games of the American League Championship Series, we had dug a 2-games-to-1 hole.

So before game four, David Ortiz, who had joined his middle-of-the-order counterpart Manny Ramirez in carrying our offense, decided it was time for a voice of reason. A players-only meeting was called.

"Hey, if we're going down, let's leave it all on the line," Ortiz said adamantly in the middle of Jacobs Field's visitors' clubhouse. "Because when you have this shirt on," he continued, grabbing his Red Sox jersey, "you're a bad motherfucker." The sight of the big designated hitter giving his proclamation did offer some comic relief, but it was also the perfect message for us to hear. All David was saying was, "Hey, we've got big games. We're highly scrutinized. We're in a city where people seem like they live and die with the results of the Red Sox. So let's lay it all on the line and let's come together as a team and do it."

Curt Schilling also chimed in, reminding us, "There was not one guy when we were down three–zero in 2004 who lost focus on what was the task at hand. And we had to go and make it as simple as possible. We had to win each pitch, we had to win each out, and then we had to win each inning. And if we did that, we put ourselves back in the game."

I thought both David and Schill nailed it. They had put things in the right perspective as we ventured into game four. So, sure enough, with all the words of wisdom still fresh in our minds, we went out and lost our third straight game and fell into a 3-games-to-1 hole. But at least these messages had put us in a better frame of mind, and with an off day before game five we seemed to still have a good grip on reality. Believe it or not, it was actually a perfect setup, allowing us to get our minds off our loss, to refocus, and realize that there's only one must-win game a year and we were standing nose to nose with it. And, just like with the Marlins, our frame of mind entering elimination games was always a bit more tolerable with Josh on the hill.

With our teammates' closed-door speeches still fresh in our memories, we came out and rode another Beckett masterpiece to a 7–1 win. It was exactly as David and Schill had said—we had to remember that we were bad motherfuckers, and then proceed to take it one out at a time. And nobody in baseball was a better reminder regarding both mandates than Josh Beckett.

While it was hard to miss Josh's mastery of another postseason, the roles of a few other teammates during our run through the playoffs also stood out in my mind. One was Schill, the forty-year-old pitcher who almost magically flipped the switch on his approach to pitching midway through the '07 season. His low-90s fastball had escaped him after a shoulder injury in the middle of June, and when he returned, a new approach had been born. He was all about location, mixing pitches, and fooling hitters. It was amazing.

Schill is the ultimate preparer, going over his videotapes incessantly. One time I told him we were about to face Texas, who had David Dellucci. Schill went back in the video room to watch footage of when he was pitching for the Phillies seven years earlier, going through all the at-bats where he faced Dellucci. I asked Curt, "Didn't you play with Dellucci after this?" He told me he had. "So," I followed up, "what are you trying to find?" Anything. He was trying to find anything he could.

Maybe it might seem like a little bit of overkill, but that's his way. That's how he prepares and I admire that.

But when it comes down to it, Curt's best attribute is an uncanny ability to execute. It makes us all feel a little more secure knowing that he is going to find a way, one method or another, even when he's not feeling his best. So it's the combination of his meticulous nature and the efficiency of his approach that really distinguishes him. And knowing he's going to put his best qualities on display at the most important times is pretty cool.

A perfect example of what Schill can do at the most important times came in game three of the American League Division Series against the Angels. You could see from the get-go that he was hitting his spots, and when the best game's best game planner is doing that, it bodes well. Similarly, when he's working away, for instance, he either hits his spot or misses by two inches, but never—never—does he miss down the middle. And that's what makes him one of the best pitchers, and best postseason pitchers, of all time. He is also a world-class fantasy football trash talker. Not fantasy football player, just talker.

We'll have our fantasy football draft and Schill will be as prepared as if he was pitching, complete with Steelers jersey. And then if he beats you, it's: "Man, you guys really played a good game. I mean, I really tip my hat to you guys. Your team really, really battled. You just came up against a better team." That's him and that's what makes him a popular guy in the clubhouse.

Schilling's incredible performance against the Angels gave us a 9–1 win and advancement into the ALCS. Curt didn't give up a run in seven innings with a fastball that lived in the high 80s. From my position at third base, it was truly a pleasure to watch. Then again, Schill wasn't alone in eliciting my amazement.

To watch David and Manny perform in that Angels series was incredible. While both had homered in the series capper, they made their presence felt from virtually the first playoff pitch. It was as if they had both just kind of cruised through the regular season and decided to pick it up to an ungodly level when the postseason came calling.

If there was a defining moment for Manny it arrived in the form of his walk-off home run in the ninth inning of game two against one of the game's premier closers, Francisco Rodriguez. I was sitting there in the on-deck circle and I found myself trying to guess along with Manny as to what Rodriguez was throwing. I would have bet the farm that he was going to offer up a slider, and I was even more certain that Manny was thinking that as well. But Rodriguez threw a fastball that stayed out over the plate and Manny just crushed it. Annihilated it. It was the longest home run I had ever seen at Fenway Park, and the view of it from the on-deck circle was stupendous.

Manny is the savant everybody says he is because he's ready for everything, and the big moment simply doesn't faze him. I thought it was pretty funny when he said in the postgame press conference, "Rodriguez is one of the best closers in the game, and I'm one of the best hitters in the game." Part of Manny being Manny is that he is brazen enough to go where others might not.

I love watching Manny hit, even in spring training. It can look like he takes three fastballs right down the middle, walks to the dugout, and doesn't bat an eye. The fact is that those three fastballs were just not part of his plan for that at-bat. But what truly amazes me about Manny as a hitter is that he has the power to hit the ball out anywhere, at any time. He suckers pitchers into his plan, knifing two or three singles to right field, and then killing that one mistake. That's what makes him such a complete hitter, that unlike guys who try to kill the ball every time, he is willing to—boom, single to right; boom, single to right; boom, double into the gap; and then when you make a mistake, boom, it's gone. It's amazing because when the rest of the baseball world tries to do that like Manny, we all find out it's not that easy. We can only marvel at how easy he makes it look.

Some people are quick to assume that Manny's relaxed vibe means he's bored with everyday baseball life. He simply comes to the park, ties up his long hair, and starts hitting home runs. It's so far from the truth. I feel fortunate that I get the chance to see the behind-the-scenes Manny, the real Manny. I watch him do his visualization drills. I see him work harder than anybody during spring-training days when most veterans are just going through the motions. He's the one yelling at me, "Lo-Lo, Lo-Lo, are we going to hit early tomorrow?" It's this quest for eternal perfection. You look at his swing and it's perfect, yet he wants to improve on his perfection.

And in the playoffs, Rodriguez and the Angels found out just how painful perfection can be.

Besides the obvious, which could be found in the game-one and game-three home runs, Manny offered another example of his quest for perfection in that Angels series. Before the first game, the position players gathered together to go through the advance scouting report on the Angels pitchers. We're not a team that typically has position players hold preseries meetings, and when we do, some guys would rather go without the information, believing that too much information can clutter your mind. But this time we understood the importance of the little things, and made sure each of the position guys was in attendance.

At the meeting we were reminded how important it was to jump all over the Angels' game-one starter, John Lackey, who had really had his problems in the past at Fenway. We were also reminded that he had a tendency to bounce balls in the dirt, resulting in wild pitches, so we should be aware of any opportunities to take the extra base. Now, Manny was sitting at this meeting, held in the batting cage behind our dugout, giving off the same relaxed vibe he always does. You would have thought he wasn't paying attention to the wild pitch portion of the presentation. As long as he drove guys in, it was all cool. But that would be selling Manny short.

In the third inning, after David Ortiz kicked off the scoring with a two-run home run, Manny drew a walk. Sure enough, Lackey bounced his third pitch to me, allowing the ball to dribble slightly away from Angels catcher Mike Napoli. Few would have blamed Manny if he played it safe and remained at first, but he was ready for such an occasion. He had listened to the scouting report. After he slid safely into second, I lofted a soft line-drive single to center, driving Manny in, which boosted our lead to 3–0. In a game that finished up at 4–0, it was a big run at the time, and it wouldn't have transpired if not for Manny's ongoing search for an edge.

As remarkable as it was to watch Manny in that Angels series, it was also remarkable to see how his achievements were enhanced by his meat-of-the-order partner in crime, Ortiz. The reason David's speech before game four in Cleveland was so effective was not just because it was a great speech but because it came from David. From him it was more than just a pep talk. David always backs up his badass lectures.

My favorite David story is from 2006, when he was facing the Texas reliever Akinori Otsuka, who was closing at the time. I came into the tunnel, behind our dugout at Fenway Park, wanting to take a look at the pitch I just got out on. We were down by two runs and David wasn't slated to head to the plate until five batters into the inning. He was down there looking at video, and he turned to me and said, "By the way, if I come up, that means I'm the winning run. And if that happens, this game is over." I looked over at Alex Cora in disbelief, and then whispered, "Yeah, whatever, dude." I knew he had done it at least five or six times, hit walk-off homers and the like, but you just don't go out and say it. Usually you do it and say nothing more than, "I had a good feeling about it." But David had no problem taking it a step further, proclaiming, "This game's over."

He turned back and continued to watch video of his last few at-bats against Otsuka, when all of a sudden, boom, someone got on, and then someone else got on, until finally he was due on deck. David got up, looked at us, and said, "See you at home plate, guys." I said to Alex, "If this guy hits a home run right now he should tell me the lotto numbers." We still weren't sold, but we didn't want to move from where the backroom televisions were for fear of jinxing something. With the delay on television we saw him hit the ball about the same time as we heard an enormous roar from the crowd. Sometimes fans will "oooh" and "aaah" for a normal fly ball, so I was still skeptical. But then Alex yelled out, "He did it!" We sprinted to the dugout and saw David was already at second base. "God, this guy is unbelievable," I said to myself. He just made this proclamation like it was nothing, just plain as day, like, "Man, these shoes are comfortable." I knew then why guys love him.

Like Schilling, like Beckett, like Manny, David is a comforting sight when the big games come around. He wants to be great, because he's already got everything. He's got money, he's got numbers, he's got strength, he's got power, and he still wants to keep hitting home runs. He still wants to be a big guy on the team. And, in the Angels series, there was nobody bigger. And knowing David was doing what he was doing on a bad knee this time around only added to the legend. He was never the type to complain about much, but he did tell me on more than one occasion, "Man, my knee is killing me." David hit .714 in the three wins over the Angels. Imagine what would have been possible without torn cartilage.

But as smooth as everything went in that Angels series, the Indians had presented us with a bumpier road. After falling into our 3-games-to-1 hole, we needed Redmond's "Push, push, push. Grind, grind, grind" chant more than ever. But after taking our day off and then watching Josh beat eventual Cy Young Award winner C. C. Sabathia in game five, we started to have a pretty good grasp on what would unlock our destiny. It wasn't thinking about having to win three straight games, because if you do that you'll usually lose the first one and the season's over. It was, as Schill pointed out in our meeting, one out at a time.

Fortunately, J. D. Drew made it a lot easier to keep our eye on the prize in game six by rocketing a two-out grand slam in the very first inning. To me, that was one of the most important hits of the postseason. The bases were loaded, nobody was out, the Cleveland starter Fausto Carmona was struggling, and both Manny and myself went down without driving in a run. We were letting this guy off the hook. But J.D. put on one of those swings I first saw in our hitting group during the first days of spring training, hitting a laser beam into the center-field bleachers. By the time three innings were complete, Carmona was long gone and we were carrying a 10–1 lead, secure that the Red Sox had finally found their way.

Three things really stood out for me in that game seven

against Cleveland. The first was the gutsy showing of our starter that night, Daisuke Matsuzaka. Daisuke appeared to be running on fumes as the final games came and went. But this time he was intent on emptying his tank, coming out with a much more aggressive approach by establishing his fastball. I think we all appreciated that. We wanted to see Daisuke throw his fastball, because he had a good one. And while he petered out after five innings—finishing his night with a strikeout of Asdrubal Cabrera on a nine-pitch at-bat—it was enough. Daisuke's effort wasn't lost on any of us.

The second thing that stood out for me that night was in the seventh inning, when Franklin Gutierrez hit a ball past me down the third-base line with Kenny Lofton at second. There was just one out, and we were clinging to a one-run lead. The ball bounced off the wall in foul ground and ricocheted out into left field. But the Cleveland third-base coach, Joel Skinner, decided to hold up Lofton, much to the shock of everybody in attendance. My first inclination was that the ball was foul, but that didn't really matter. As far as Lofton being held up, I couldn't blame Skinner too much, considering I have seen so many balls carry off that wall and go right to the shortstop. I understood the process.

Think about it: If Lofton had gotten thrown out, then it was two outs, runner at first, and it would have been a rally killer. Instead, you had runners on first and third with one out and Casey Blake up, a guy who runs pretty well, makes good contact, and presents a good chance of getting the run in. But it didn't work out for Skinner or the Indians, as Blake hit a ground ball to me, I flipped it over to Dustin, and he finished off our biggest double play of the season.

That was classic postseason. You're in a big game, with all these replays, and everyone is second-guessing when things don't go right. If Blake hit a double, nobody would be talking about Joel Skinner. I'm sure he regrets it now, but I can't really say it was the wrong decision at the time from where I was standing.

What was not up for debate—and what really stood out for me that night—was what came around in the bottom of that inning. With Jacoby Ellsbury having reached on an error by Blake—a tough time for a good player—Petie came up and plopped a game-altering two-run homer just over the left-field wall. With six outs to go before our invitation to the World Series, it allowed for a 5–2 lead, just the cushion we needed. But where the hit truly separated itself was in Petie's reaction. He watched the ball and then did a little bat flip, although I was sure the bat was going to flip his five feet seven inches. It was a big moment, a huge hit, but when you bat flip you had better hit the ball ten rows deep, at least. This ball went about three feet over the wall. I told him later that he had better thank God that it went over the fence, because after that display I think I would have run all the way to second base and punched him right in the mouth. But once again, it was pure Pedroia, and we loved it.

It was the perfect way to punch our ticket to Colorado.

But when the World Series began we came to realize that being the favorite is not easy. I understood firsthand the benefits of playing the role of the underdog from my experience in '03, and we knew that even though Colorado was the hottest team on the planet they would be carrying a good measure of the "nothing to lose" attitude. If we had lost to Cleveland, however, I don't think people would have said, "Man, maybe they let this one go," because the reality was that the Indians had two guys that were close to being twenty-game winners, we won the same number of games during the season, and they had beaten the Yankees in the previous round. With the Rockies, people truly thought we were the better team. So there was a lot of pressure. But the one thing we did have on our side was momentum, especially considering Colorado was coming in with eight days off.

And once Petie lofted Rockies starter Jeff Francis's second pitch of the game over the left-field wall for yet another home run (this one sans stare and bat flip), there was a pretty good feeling we were on our way.

We were.

CHAPTER SIX

The Game of a Lifetime

Journal entry, October 29, 2007

"Unbelievable!!!"

_I_ looked to the right of me. There was my wife, Bertica, a woman who had given me a lifetime of support. Since that first date in high school, she had been guiding me through the saga of my life.

To the left of me sat our new friend, the World Series MVP trophy. This was the reward, for both of us.

It was hard to look into the silver reflection of the trophy and not see all my life's ups and downs staring back. I saw Cuba, the cancer, the comeback. And even somewhat more diminutive memories. It was this piece of metal, after all, that at one time stood between me and hundreds of thousands of dollars. Nine years earlier I was told that the only way I wouldn't go from living life as a $13,000-a-year minor leaguer to the starting third baseman for the New York Yankees was if Scott Brosius, the team's incumbent at the position, was holding the World Series MVP trophy at the conclusion of the 1998 World Series. And by the end of the series, the trophy was his.

So you might understand why, until this October 28, 2007, night in Colorado, I viewed the award with a hint of irony.

The trophy and I had now become well acquainted. Its presence stretched out the euphoria of our World Series–clinching game-four 4–3 win over the Rockies and carried all those glorious memories. Not just the memories of our victory, but memories from the course of my life that came flooding back during the ten-minute bus ride back to the hotel from Coors Field.

It was the culmination of a postseason that had been all about self-reflection. As I told Bertica at the beginning of my first playoff run with the Red Sox, I was determined to soak in every beautiful moment this time around. When I won the World Series with the Marlins in '03, it was all so new and I didn't have a chance to really savor every moment.

As I told my wife, this time it was going to be different— and it was.

As I sat in the bus with Bertica, I thought back to what my dad had told me when I was eight years old. "If you want to be in that situation and you try your best, good things are going to happen." Never were there truer words spoken, and the latest "good thing" was the most satisfying of all, the most memorable home-run trot of my career.

Unlike my Little League game winner, the home run I hit that night in Colorado found a fence to go over. And, okay, maybe rounding the bases after giving your team a 3–0 lead in the seventh inning of the decisive game of the World Series might offer a bit more of a rush than the ball that came off my aluminum bat a quarter of a century earlier.

And believe it or not, that World Series hit had been predicted by my brother Victor. Just minutes before I tore into the pitch from Colorado starting pitcher Aaron Cook, Victor turned to one of my best friends, Garo Friguls, and said, "To me, Mike has the 'M' and the 'V,' and if he hits a home run here I will give him the 'P.' I think he's going to get the 'P' right here." Wow. Nobody knows me better than Victor.

But not even my younger brother could have imagined the exact chain of remarkable events that began with breakfast the morning of game four and concluded two days later on a duck boat in Boston.

When I woke up the morning of game four, I felt, as I think we all did, like we were on the brink of something great. We could feel a championship on our fingertips, although nobody would say as much. Baseball players are a superstitious lot and, 3--games-to-0 lead or not, going about our business was the only way to proceed. For me, the first few moments of what ultimately became one of the best days of my life were spent sorting out my schedule for the next few hours. Cook hadn't pitched in a while and my plan was to get to the park early so as to become as familiar with this guy as humanly possible. This is something I can only do on the actual day that I am to take on each respective hurler—never before. I know who's going to pitch games one, two, three, and four, but I'm never going to jump ahead. It has to be fresh in my mind, and Cook, a right-hander with a mean sinking fastball, was the task at hand on this day.

I planned to make my way over from the hotel to arrive at the park at about eleven thirty in the morning, more than five hours before the first pitch. My approach was all about limiting risks. The day of the game offered no certainties, as our second baseman, Dustin Pedroia, found out the day before. Petie is one of my favorite guys on our team, thanks in part to the piss and vinegar that usually emanate from his five-foot-seven body. So when a Coors Field security guard tried to refuse Pedroia admittance into his place of work, it wasn't going to be a pretty scene. But I'd say the guard got off fairly easy.

For Petie it wasn't complicated. "Why don't you ask Jeff Francis who I am?" Pedroia said, not breaking stride as the guard attempted to figure out what had just happened. The guy might have not known what Petie looked like, but he most certainly was familiar with one of Dustin's recent accomplishments—a leadoff home run against Francis, Colorado's starter in the first game of the World Series.

Whether it was a misguided security guard, a traffic jam, or anything else, I was going to limit my risks and get to Coors plenty early. If there's one thing my journey has taught me, it's to not take anything for granted.

But baseball and downtime are always inseparable, no matter how early you arrive at the ballpark. That's where Victor stepped in to do his part.

Vic is four years younger than I am, and doesn't possess the height of either me or my older brother, Carlos, but, I'll tell you what, he might be the best athlete of all of us. It's almost a shame he never had my frame, because he would have probably become much better than I. Other than the physical stature, we have always been similar, more so than any of our other siblings. He's athletic, often flying by the seat of his pants, but he is still very intelligent. Vic is also very serious when need be. Leading up to the fourth game of the World Series, intensity was the order of the day, but so was some good-natured brotherly bonding.

Up until it was time to make my entrance on Coors Field, I decided to join Victor in tending to the business that was planning for life after the '07 season, more specifically my family's off-season vacation. In two months my family and I were heading up to Spokane, Washington, to spend New Year's with my old teammate Mike Redmond. I had heard about the bad weather in the Northwest, and having grown up in South Florida, I wasn't going to be unprepared. So, while Bertica joined the other wives in constructing World Series T-shirts (not my idea of a good World Series distraction), Victor and I went over to NikeTown to find some rain gear. Shopping in the fan-crazed chaos that comes with playing in Boston can be tricky, but I thought blending in might be a bit more manageable within the Denver city limits. Not so.

All of the store's patrons that day were grabbing free Colorado Rockies skullcaps, except for Victor and me, of course. A local camera crew eventually spotted me wandering around the store, and started to trail us. They were dying to see if we were going to buy any of the Rockies gear that made up a good majority of the store's inventory. Every time I touched a Rockies jacket, I could feel the camera lens bear down on me. We had to leave. But before we exited, my brother started creeping over to where the free merchandise was being distributed. His goal was to try to make good on the promise of taking one of the caps, putting it on his head, and then watching it intentionally fall off, so as to have the cameras film him stomping all over the Rockies' logo. Thankfully, my brother chose to take the path of least resistance.

Once we were out of the store, I turned to my brother and asked, "Do you think we should go back in?" I was annoyed that our simple shopping outing had been compromised. Thankfully, my brother brought me back to reality. "Well, if you really think NikeTown is going to give us the victory, let's do it." We both knew the answer. It was time to get ready for the game.

Half a day later, it was time to reap the benefits from a day, and lifetime, of preparation.

The feeling of hitting home runs was only introduced to me fairly late in my baseball-playing life. By the completion of my junior year at Coral Gables High, I was still hitting ninth and was the proud owner of one extra-base hit, a double. But by the time I stepped into the batter's box against Cook in the seventh inning of game four, I had figured out a few things when it came to the process of hitting the ball over outfielders' heads.

Hitting the long ball is largely about muscle and skill, as I came to know all too well in those days of settling for singles. But unlocking the riddle that is the pitcher's approach is what often makes the greatest difference ultimately between frustration and glory.

In this case, there were a few things I knew to be true about my opponent. Cook was a good sinker-slider guy who always pitched well at Coors Field. I remember watching film of him before game four and thinking that he was very effective with his sinker at his home park, and by the time the seventh came around he hadn't disappointed, pounding me with sinkers in my first at-bat.

Most pitchers work the middle of the plate and away on me, which is the pitchers' approach on 90 percent of hitters anyway—that is, unless they have an above-average sinker, like Cook has. I grounded out on my first at-bat, when he found the inside part of the plate on each of the two pitches, and then hit a double on the first pitch in my second time up. So now I was thinking that maybe he was going to keep going inside, because some pitchers think that the hitter is thinking, *He did it once, so he's not going to do it again.* Or maybe the pitcher is thinking, *Now that he hit that pitch, he's going to look for another pitch.*

Now you can start to understand why Ted Williams once said that hitting a baseball is the hardest thing to do in sports.

It was my third at-bat—usually the time the hitter-pitcher dynamic becomes mostly mental—and the first pitch came, another fastball in. In my mind I was thinking he was going to come right back to it. So I looked for a sinker in and there it was.

One of my strengths has always been that when a ball is in, if I keep my hands inside the right way, I can hit a ball that might be a little off the plate fair. I've been able to do that a lot. I remember my Triple-A coach Stump Merrill saying when he would throw me batting practice, "You know those are balls inside and you keep them fair." So that has always stuck in my head, that maybe sometimes I can get a little closer to the plate than a normal guy and cut down the outside part of the plate, which has always been a weakness for me.

The inside sinker I was looking for this time actually was a little bit down in the strike zone, but when you're looking for it, it's less of a surprise. I knew I hit it really well, with nice trajectory, but at that point I didn't take anything for granted because it was the World Series. I was looking at the left fielder and saw him running and subsequently slow down. That is a great feeling. But what I really, really enjoyed was that home-run trot, especially since I had never hit a home run in the World Series.

I previously owned a couple of home runs in the playoffs—some big ones, to boot—but after guessing right against Cook, and then getting to jog around the bases, nothing compared. My first thought was to look up at the four people who received my stash of complimentary tickets, Bertica, my younger brother, Victor, and two of my best friends, Alex Garcia and Garo Friguls. But, as obvious as it may sound, making sure I touched the bases became the priority.

Then I came back to the dugout and it was like Little League all over again. Usually when guys hit a big home run, a few teammates, such as David Ortiz or sometimes Julio Lugo, will be at the top step. This time there were twenty guys serving as the welcome wagon, each and every one feeling how close we were to winning this thing.

We knew two of baseball's best relief pitchers, Hideki Okajima and Jonathan Papelbon, were in our bullpen. We were in the seventh, up by three runs, and just nine outs from a championship. All I could think about was what could be happening in the next hour.

This was the moment I had yearned for ever since that car ride with Dad. To be on the big stage at the big moment. It was also the culmination of years of what I call my visualizations.

Before each game I'll rest for twenty minutes, just visualizing what is going to happen. I see this as helping make the transition from "what might be" to "what is" that much more natural. I focus on seeing the face of the pitcher I'm going against that day, the pitch from him, and the situations with guys on base. I want to feel like when I go into the batter's box I've already done it so there is only one more part to do, and that is the physical part. If you get into the box and you're wondering whether you are going to be able to succeed in that particular situation, without having visualized it before, I think you're just distracting yourself.

While the thought of what I might do when the final out of the World Series arrived might not have been at the forefront of this pregame routine, the circumstances I found myself in for the final innings weren't all that foreign. It's all about finding a certain comfort level, and that was something I started to learn how to do all the way back in high school.

Back at Coral Gables High School, we would jog about a mile to Doctors Hospital, where our team was to serve as the guinea pigs for the residents' shoulder programs, tests, and things of that sort. It was a trade-off, our bodies for their weight room. Once a week, after lifting weights, we met with one of their guys in an aerobic room that was made up of wood floors and mirrored walls. He asked us to all lie down, close our eyes, and listen to some kind of beach music. We were all looking at one another thinking this guy was some kind of weirdo.

So this guy told us he didn't want us to visualize our next opponent, but rather the image of him pitching to us. He wanted us to see the ball actually coming out of his fingers, to see the red stitching, and then he asked us to imagine his best pitch, the one that would be the toughest for us to hit. The idea was to picture yourself hitting that pitch hard, in the exact place where you would want to hit it. Sure, this experience was a little strange at first, but I'll tell you what: I started using this mental exercise more and more in high school, and then college, and kept on doing it all the way until there were nine outs standing in the way of a world championship.

I might have taken these visualizations a little more seriously in the bigger games or moments, but when you're a member of the Red Sox those scenarios aren't usually hard to find. Earlier in the '07 season we were facing the Yankees (a game that would fall under the "big game" classification even if it was played on a sandlot in December). I had never faced their highly touted rookie pitcher Joba Chamberlain, but I did watch him on film throw an explosive fastball and slider and tried to focus on those images leading into that game.

So in my first at-bat I wanted to be ready for that fastball, but he threw me a slider, which was a ball. He came back with a fastball, which I fouled back. But the radar gun reading was at 98 miles per hour, so now I was thinking I was on a 98-mile-per-hour fastball, so we were there. He then threw a slider, which I could see he was striking out a lot of guys on. I stayed on it and hit a single up the middle.

So in that case, even though I was unfamiliar with Joba, I still tried to visualize and put myself in a position where I saw his pitch before I actually faced him. I could have grounded out to short, and I might have lined out to third, but the fact was that I pictured myself staying through the ball and my preparation had really helped me. It might not work for everybody, but it works for me.

No amount of pregame visualization, however, could have prepared me for the glorious final moments of game four. No, that was a full-fledged dream of a lifetime.

By the time the ninth inning rolls around, all you want is easy outs. Thankfully, the first batter, Colorado's Yorvit Torrealba, grounded out to Dustin Pedroia at second base. The second guy up was Jamey Carroll, whom I had talked to Pedroia about earlier in the game, saying, "Man, this guy's a pretty good player. He always seems to put the bat on the ball and he can hit a fastball." Right on cue, Carroll laid into one. I just looked at Jacoby Ellsbury go back in left field with a lump in my throat, thinking, *Please don't go out.* We were up by one run, leading 4–3, but when it comes to putting the punctuation on a world championship, you don't want to leave anything to chance. Then, boom! Ells catches it at the wall. One to go.

Now I was thinking, like probably most everybody else, that with Pap on the mound and just one out left there was no way we were going to lose. I just wanted a little pop-up, a weak grounder, anything like that.

On the sixth pitch Pap reared back and threw a fastball right down the middle, which the Rockies' final batter, Seth Smith, swung through. That was it! Hands went up in the air, players and coaches converged from all angles to storm the mound, and the celebration began.

Once again, my first inclination was to look up to the family section, where Bertica, Victor, Garo, and Alex were sitting. To understand why acknowledging these people was my priority, you have to realize how much my family and group of friends have meant in navigating this journey. So before running to join my teammates for the traditional pitching mound pig pile, I turned, looked up, and celebrated for a few seconds with my support system from a hundred yards away.

Obviously my family is the foundation, but Alex and Garo were two of six guys I have been unbelievably tight with since we were all eight years old—those two, Eddy Garcia, Alex's brother, Leo Leon, Andy Fernandez, whom we will forever know as the eighth-grade MVP, and Joche Espin. There was a time we all went our separate ways, going off to play college ball and start our professional lives, but eventually everybody filtered back. Our friendship started on the Coral Gables' Wiffle ball fields and has lasted right through two World Series.

In fact, the reason Alex and Garo were in Colorado was because they were the only ones not there when I joined the Florida Marlins in clinching the title back in '03 at Yankee Stadium. Believe me, for those four years in between, those two were officially declassified as fans for their lack of attendance at the clincher. But when this playoff run came to a head, Garo was all over the place, saying, "I'm not missing Colorado for anything." And when it was all said and done, not only had my two friends regained their status as faithful World Series followers, but they also found themselves with the upper hand.

The very first call from Garo to the others? "Yeah, you guys might have been there when they won before, but we were standing on the field holding the World Series MVP trophy." And, just for good measure, the first thing both of those guys did when we got back to the party was e-mail pictures of themselves in the heart of the on-field celebration, with the trophy and the big smiles that went with it.

The bottom line is that I'm incredibly lucky to have those guys. I'm so spoiled, because on top of two brothers and a sister I'm close to, I've got these friends who are second to none. They help ground me and that allows me to enjoy other things. I've always said that I play baseball but that's not who I am. That's part of who I am. But I'd much rather be a good father, husband, friend, and brother. That is really important to me, along with baseball. The game is just what everyone sees, but there is so much more to me.

That's what made the moments that night, after we got the final out, so special. The phone call with my parents, my wife sitting by my side, and friends and teammates there ready to reminisce.

No doubt, having representatives come up from Major League Baseball after you win a World Series and tell you that you are the proud owner of two new cars is pretty cool. But even that doesn't eclipse something as simple as the sight of Victor. In the chaos of the postgame celebration I looked over and he was standing there wearing a Christopher Walken T-shirt that read, "I got the fever!" a catchphrase from a *Saturday Night Live* skit. Then I looked again and saw he had painted big eyebrows and a goatee on Walken's face, and in between "the fever," had written "Red Sox."

"What's wrong with you, man?" I asked him jokingly.

He was just like, "Hey, there's no other time to do it. There's no other day I'll get away with this." Fair enough.

To see those guys jumping up and down, hugging people, getting a chance to hold the trophy . . . man, all I can say is that when your brother, your wife, and two of your best friends tell you that they're proud of you, there is no better feeling.

It gave me a happy glow that wasn't about to go away anytime soon, although the one part of the sensation that I was trying to shake by the time we got back to the hotel room that night was the numbness in my arms. It doesn't dawn on you until nobody is around, but holding the World Series MVP trophy for three straight hours isn't light lifting.

I guess it was understandable that the weariness didn't

kick in until I had to find a resting spot for the trophy back at the hotel. When you're standing on a baseball field in front of thousands of people chanting, "MVP, MVP," "Re-sign Lowell," and even "Don't sign A-Rod," all directly at you, well, that's as powerful as it is surreal.

The fact is, I wasn't thinking about all that stuff. I was just in the moment. Sure, I recognized the extraordinary honor of being identified as the most valued player on baseball's biggest stage. And, thanks to Peter Gammons's postgame message, I had come into the information that Alex Rodriguez—my former double-play partner for the Christopher Columbus High School junior varsity team—would be joining me on the free-agent market. But I wasn't really focusing on these specifics.

There is no question that I would rather go 0 for 20 but win the World Series. That would be fine. But to get this outpouring of support, it was something I didn't expect. I literally felt like I was floating and everyone was chanting for somebody else.

Even in all my visualizations, that was something I never imagined. Neither was having to worry about finding a hiding place for the World Series MVP trophy later that night in my hotel room.

Everything about that night, in fact, was hard to fathom. Here I was, tucking away this trophy before maid service came in so I could go down to a party where I would be celebrating a World Series victory with everybody from Pedroia to the actress Rene Russo. I couldn't believe how far I had come.

213

In particular, I remember a conversation I had that night with Josh Beckett. It held special significance, because the reality is that I wouldn't have been there if it wasn't for Josh.

We had gone through the tough times with the Marlins, then the jubilation that came with winning the Series in '03, and finally the trade to Boston that, in my mind, solidified a bond that will last forever.

"Man," he said, "we've got to get to the playoffs more often, because every time we're in we win."

John Henry, the principal owner of the Red Sox, who served in the same capacity with the Marlins for much of my time there, came by and said, "I guess this was a pretty good trade for you two. We've pulled two World Series MVPs out of it. Maybe we'll have to have a battle between you two for who's going to get it next."

"No problem," I said. "Let's just get there again and we'll do it."

From day one the thing I loved about Josh, even when he was just nineteen years old in his first spring-training game with the Marlins, was that he had that killer instinct. He just wanted to embarrass the hitter. Sure, it might have been a little bit brash at the beginning, especially when he might have felt better about striking out three guys in twenty-one pitches than about getting three outs in five pitches. But he had that fire in him, and that's what I really liked about him.

And he is a really nice guy off the field. He might not seem like it when you see him on the road, but that's just him. A lot of pitchers are like that. They are very different the day they pitch. But, believe me, this is a great guy.

And his path to this point wasn't easy, either. He went through some really tough times in '06, when I think some unrealistic expectations were put on him, just like what happened to me in '05. But this season I could see that Josh had entered into another level of his career.

A huge part of Josh's maturation process was the simple fact that he wasn't living and dying with the strikeout. When I think about him as a younger pitcher with the Marlins, there is one instance that I always remember. It was this one game against the Arizona Diamondbacks when he got a one-two-three inning, but all were rockets, a line out to second, a line out to center, and a line out to right. He came in the dugout and was just cursing and throwing his glove. We were all thinking how weird it was. But that was part of his mentality. He simply didn't want guys to make good contact.

So the baseball gods obviously listened to that and then, a couple of innings later, the Diamondbacks hit three straight home runs off of him. Needless to say, I think he appreciates outs much more now.

Flash forward to this season. After meeting these unrealistic expectations by figuring it all out and turning in an unbelievable season in '07, he came face-to-face with another round of sky-high expectations. We got to the playoffs, he was coming off this Cy Young–caliber year, so everybody put two and two together and suggested he should automatically repeat what I thought was the best stretch of pitching I had ever seen, during the '03 postseason.

In a big market like Boston everything quickly becomes very black-and-white. Everybody wants to know, was '03 a fluke, and if it wasn't, is this guy really that kind of horse? So what does Josh do? He throws another crate of unfair expectations out the window and becomes an even more dominant pitcher in the '07 playoffs. I didn't think it was possible, but he did it. And because he did, here we were sitting in some room at four o'clock in the morning, looking back nostalgically at how we arrived at such a place.

Believe me, there are a lot of guys who have talent comparable to Josh's, with just electric stuff. But mentally they are so far behind because they don't want to be that big guy. When Dad told me in the car on the way back from Little League that I should want to be that guy who wants to be in the big moment, he was talking about being like Josh Beckett.

That's why, when it came time for me to move to an entirely different league and team, like I did when the Red Sox took me on in late November 2005, I was glad it was with a guy like Josh in a place like Boston.

I remembered how I ended up in this happy situation. At first, when rumors started circulating that the Marlins were looking to start blowing up the roster in '05, it seemed like a long shot. The first word I heard that year was regarding a deal that would have sent me and A. J. Burnett to Baltimore at the trading deadline. They would get Burnett, probably the most coveted pitcher at the deadline that season, but Baltimore would also have to take me and my contract.

It had come to this, where, because of an '05 season in which I hit .236 with eight home runs and the fact that I would be making $9 million in each of the next two seasons, my services had become a necessary evil. But, in the case of the Orioles, it wasn't a sacrifice they were willing to make, partly because their current third baseman, Melvin Mora, had a deal that ran through '06.

Then, after the season, I started hearing word that a deal might be close where the Texas Rangers would be getting me and Josh. I called him up and he was pumped. "How great would that be?" he said, being a born-and-bred Texan. "Sure," I said, "great for you."

The more I thought about it, however, the more I didn't mind the idea. The Rangers had some good players, and their home field, the Ballpark at Arlington, is a hitter's park, and I hadn't really played in a hitter's park for my home field before. So I was curious, to say the least.

Then, almost as suddenly as the Texas rumors faded away, the Red Sox came into view. I think that when the Red Sox heard the Rangers thing was falling apart, they jumped in. From my perspective, the prospect of playing in Boston was pretty much out of nowhere, but, as was the case with Texas, I soon saw it as an appealing potential destination. Back in 1997 the Red Sox made a trade with the Yankees (the last one between the two rivals to this day), with Mike Stanley going to New York and Tony Armas and Jim Mecir coming to Boston. A few days later the Yankees' minor-league coordinator came up to me and said, "You have no idea how close you were to being traded to the Red Sox."

I remember thinking that wouldn't have been such a bad thing. I was always a dead pull, right-handed hitter, and everybody said that left-field wall was really close. So, even up until the time the Red Sox rumblings kicked up in '05, I had this idea that of all the parks that might cater to my swing and hitting approach, Fenway Park might be the best. In the days leading up to Thanksgiving '05, I discovered I was going to get a chance to find out if my instincts were correct.

One of my agents, Seth Levinson, called to tell me it was a done deal. Josh and I were going to Boston for four minor leaguers. My first two emotions were relief and excitement. The relief stemmed from knowing that there would be no more hypothetical e-mails to answer, and the excitement came from my being headed to a contending team and a park that fit my swing. I went on to hit .317 at Fenway Park over the next two years, so that's one assessment I think I might have nailed.

Could I have imagined that it was going to be such a perfect fit in Boston? Predicting what happened at the end of the '07 season would have challenged Nostradamus. But it happened and now was our time to celebrate. I had fourteen relatives flying and driving in for a dinner at Abe & Louie's before jumping on a duck boat for the championship parade.

It was nice to have the four pieces of my support system in Colorado, but now my parents and the rest of the Lowell family tree were in town for a whole new round of merriment. As weird as it might sound, the first thing I asked my dad when I saw him was what they were saying on TV, because those are the things we don't hear.

"They showed nine different replays of your slide home!" I still wasn't used to seeing him so visibly excited. "And ten different replays of Bobby Kielty shooting his arms up after he went deep. And then they showed every angle of Papelbon known to mankind." Dad just kept going on and on, not allowing the smile to leave his face once.

While the parade through the streets of Boston was two days after the World Series clincher, our excitement level was still high by the time we loaded up on the amphibious vehicles they use for the event. Two months earlier I had taken my family on the duck boats to celebrate my daughter's sixth birthday, but this time the kids were in for a more chaotic experience. For the next two and a half hours, as we rode around the city that had been my happy home for two years now, we were bombarded by raucous chants from spectators.

"MVP!"

"Re-sign Lowell!"

The shouts never stopped from the time we pulled out of Van Ness Street until I drove away from the Fenway Park parking lot for the final time in '07. It was unbelievable. Here were fans who eat, sleep, and drink baseball, and they were showing me their ultimate support by saying they wanted me back. And then I had the image of Jason Varitek in the duck boat in front of us and the picture had officially been painted.

Tek is not only the captain of the team but one of the most

well-respected, hardworking guys around. Everybody admires how he prepares for a baseball game. But this time, he uncharacteristically let his guard down. Somebody handed him up a sign that read, "Re-sign Lowell." And for the remainder of the parade he was waving this piece of cardboard, encouraging the sidewalks upon sidewalks of Red Sox fans to repeat the message strewn across the poster. That, well, that was it. That was the exclamation point.

Fans can love you, upper management can love you, but if you don't get along with your teammates, you don't have much. Getting that kind of endorsement, from the captain of the team, it was something extraspecial.

For that entire two hours, riding through the streets of Boston, I continuously turned to Bertica, uttering what became a repetitive message: "This is awesome." When it was all said and done, we had more than two hundred pictures on my wife's camera, pictures full of people holding homemade signs encouraging my return. But even those images couldn't compare to what was stored in my mind's eye. The signs, the chants, the love.

Everybody has their story, their own roller-coaster ride. What I held on to as I stepped down from the duck boat was that my journey was made possible because of perspective. You can choose to harp on the negativity—I certainly could have when cancer came calling, or when the hits were hard to find in 2005—but if you choose the positive you're going to get the most out of life.

It has worked for me, and I'm not about to stop now.

Epilogue

Journal entry, January 22, 2008

I am sitting in my hotel room after having had
dinner with President Bush and the First Lady. What
a unique evening. A baseball-themed dinner with
six other players and their spouses, as well as Tito
and his wife. We had a very casual dinner and
talked baseball, no politics. We all even got to walk
into the Oval Office. I started thinking as I was in
there among all the historical paintings and artifacts
just how demanding his job must be with everything going on in the world. It was so refreshing to
hear him speak about not forgetting his Texas roots
and how he has used his faith to help him in some
tough decisions. I know that even if I was guaranteed a 100 percent election vote in my favor, I would
not want his job. So having dinner with the most
influential or powerful man in the world was definitely an experience to treasure. Not a bad perk for
being on a world-champion team.

    This gets me to thinking. What an unbelievable
off-season it has been. I re-signed with the team I
love, we are reigning world champs, and the family
is great. Alexis keeps learning and is reading now.
She is so cute when she shows me how much she is

reading. I love picking her up from school and asking her how her day was and she responds, "Super," meaning she got a superstar for perfect behavior and work on a chart.

Anthony took a little longer to adjust to the school thing, but he has really come around, to the point of telling me, "Go," when we get to his pre-school classroom. They both love being outside and are always asking me to jump on the trampoline with them or ride bikes or go in the pool. I think that is what I love most about them. Never really wanting to sit in front of a TV like vegetables unless they are tired. Bertica is really excited for this upcoming season. We bought a place of our own in the city and can't wait to make it "homey." I love the fact that she likes Boston—it makes things so much easier.

Easily the biggest surprise of the off-season was the fan mail. Every year Mom organizes it and sets it up for me to sign, and this year was no different. Almost 99 percent of the mail is requests to sign things and mail back. However, this year as Mom was organizing she wrote me a letter expressing how taken aback she was by the number of letters expressing congratulations and thanks. No signature, no request for money, just sincere congratulations and thanks. As I read my mom's letter my feelings echoed what she found. What unbelievable fans we have. I was moved by the fact that so many people took the time to deliver a message that came from the heart. That right there solidified in my mind that I am in the perfect baseball place. Great teammates, great coaches, great fans, and a happy family. That, my friends, is something money cannot buy. I will leave on this note. I can't wait for '08. A true chance to defend a hard-earned title and start another journey. Unbelievable that we are less than four weeks away. Overall life is still good. Check that, life is great . . . ML.

I had been to the White House when we won the World Series in 2003, but this was different. This was, in my view, a personal invitation.

I was the guest of President George Bush and his wife, Laura, joining six other baseball players along with our manager, Terry Francona, for a formal dinner. Life as the World Series MVP was turning out to be pretty good. Here I was, sitting three seats away from the president of the United States, talking about stadiums, pitchers, and a variety of other subjects. I even got to ask the First Lady if there was, indeed, a button they could push any time of the day to get any kind of food they desired. I was told there wasn't.

The visit to Pennsylvania Avenue was the capper for what had been a great off-season. I had been the grand marshal for the Disney World parade, gotten the chance to give a postgame talk to a Division I basketball team, and was now asking the leader of the free world where the White House poker room was.

And, of course, there was the matter of my contract.

To be honest, the one thing I hadn't spent a whole lot of time thinking about was life beyond the chants and the signs at our parade. I was also hoping they would "re-sign Lowell," but in the back of my mind I knew the public's adoration wasn't where I should be looking. I needed to see the love coming from the Red Sox decision makers, and I suspected that the process of uncovering that affection might officially end this fairy tale and bring me back to reality—baseball was still a business.

Our manager, Terry Francona, had dropped in a "I hope you re-sign" here and there, and part of me felt he wouldn't be doing that if there wasn't some desire on the club's behalf to get a deal done.

Still, I was content to let the World Series euphoria linger as long as possible before diving into the world of contracts and negotiations. Unfortunately, I had about four days after the parade before pushing aside the World Series MVP trophy, and the memories that went with it, to start focusing in on business.

The first time I talked about any sort of strategy regarding my impending free agency was in June, when I met up with my agents, Sam and Seth Levinson, in New York. At that point I was having a pretty good year, staying healthy, and was shaping up to be one of the few everyday third basemen slated to hit the open market. As the Levinsons explained, position-wise everything goes in cycles (the demand for pitching, on the other hand, is a constant), and this time around the majority of the established third basemen were too young or locked into major-league deals already. Eric Chavez, Scott Rolen, Aramis Ramirez, Adrian Beltre, all of those guys.

Seth said, "There are really only two everyday third basemen who will be up for free agency. Obviously, Alex Rodriguez is one of them, but he's in another stratosphere statistically. So, outside of Alex, it's you and Pedro Feliz, and your numbers are better than Pedro Feliz's, so I would put you ahead of him."

He went on to explain that on top of the lack of competition in the open market, most of the suitors could very well be big-market teams, such as the Angels, Dodgers, Red Sox, possibly Houston, and the Yankees if Alex was going to utilize the clause in his contract, opt out, and enter free agency. "If Alex opts out," Seth said, "you're going to have the Red Sox and Yankees, and that's the greatest thing in the world." In the world of baseball agents, pitting the Red Sox against the Yankees, and vice versa, is the best negotiating ammunition of all. Nothing comes close.

"I believe we can get maybe a three-year, thirty-million-dollar deal," Seth summarized. That, in my mind, was sweet music. I had made $9 million in each of the last two years, but that was only because my contract was back-loaded, with the first two years coming at significantly less. Ten million for each of three years would be a dream.

The client-agent dynamic in the world of professional sports is a strange one. You are forced to put your faith, and career, in the hands of somebody other than yourself, and for any kind of athlete that is foreign territory. But I trusted both Sam and Seth, and have since the day I met them back in '97.

I had reached Triple-A and figured it was time to get an agent. I had this one guy for about a month before a couple of my teammates who were with the Levinsons, including my former high school buddy Eli Marrero and Cliff Floyd, suggested I have lunch with Sam and Seth. The day I was to meet with them I hit two home runs and Cliff hit two home runs, so before a word was said, Sam was feeling pretty good about himself.

Sam showed up and he had these two laptops with all this info. He said, "What do you think you will hit in the big leagues?"

I told him, "I think I can hit .290."

So he responded, "Let's put .280." The questions continued.

"How many home runs do you think you can hit?" he asked.

"Probably twenty-five," I said.

Sam said, "Let's put twenty. How many runs will you drive in?"

"I should drive in ninety runs a year," was my response.

He said, "Let's put eighty. Okay, we have .280, twenty home runs, and eighty RBIs. How many third basemen in the league have averaged that over the last five years? The answer is six, and here are their salaries."

Sam went on to point out that the Yankees, whom I was still

with at the time, had signed this huge deal with Adidas, so Nike would overpay prospects, like myself. Here I was making $13,000 for the year and he was saying I could get $10,000 from some company to wear the same batting gloves I was wearing anyway. It was unbelievable.

Sam then showed me some of the contracts of his guys who were in the minor leagues and what they were making. I instantly asked, "Are you showing me this or are you guaranteeing me this?" He said that if I signed with them he would guarantee a deal within two days. Now I had to check this out with my current guy.

I called my agent at the time and said, "What's your take on maybe calling Nike or Mizuno or Wilson about a glove deal, or maybe wearing their spikes or batting gloves? I heard that Nike might be willing to pay prospects."

His response was, "Mike, if you need a thousand dollars I'll just give it to you." Right there I knew I had to write a letter and fire him.

Now, ten years later, Sam and Seth were guiding me toward a contract of a lifetime, which was only getting better as the season, and my numbers, progressed. (By mid-September the statistics had remained strong, with my insertion into the cleanup spot during Manny Ramirez's absence, and the number-five hole upon his return.) With just a few weeks remaining in the regular season, I met up with the Levinsons once more, taking the next step in formulating an off-season strategy.

"Where do you want to go?" Seth asked flat out.

"I want to play in Boston. There's no doubt about it," I responded.

The problem, as he explained it, was that the Red Sox might come up short in terms of the number of years, which I couldn't really comprehend, because if they did want me they certainly had the money to reach an acceptable level.

"That's just the way things are," Seth said. "They're going to give me the stats, you're thirty-three and you're going to play the next year at thirty-four, and so forth and so on. But I can guarantee this: You're going to get at least three for thirty million dollars somewhere, and I think we can get four years from some teams." He had talked briefly with the Red Sox general manager, Theo Epstein, in New York at the end of August, but only to gauge each side's interest. The dynamic was changing, and with only a few weeks left in the season, it didn't seem like the projections were going anywhere.

Four years. Who wouldn't want that extra year? And it could get even better. How about if we made a run through the postseason? Keeping the pieces of a winner is always a more viable scenario. I would talk shop with Sam and Seth one more time, the off day after we fell behind 3 games to 1 in Cleveland, but after that it would have to wait. So it did, until four days after I got off the duck boat.

Even though the Red Sox had fifteen days to exclusively negotiate with me following the World Series win, it was probably smart on both sides to wait a bit, because emotion was still such a huge factor. I think Seth might have asked for the stars, the moon, the clouds, and then the sun, and maybe have

God send down a little blessing as well. He was convinced I could get four years guaranteed at between $50 million and $60 million. When I heard that, I went crazy, absolutely crazy! To think where I came from and to have this kind of money landing at my doorstep—clearly the dream hadn't ended upon leaving Coors Field.

All of the numbers were nice, but I still wanted to play in Boston. The only thing that might change my mind was if the Red Sox came in with a two-year offer, because then I would not only be passing up on twice the money, but it would also suggest they didn't really want me.

Then came the first offer from the Sox: three years, $36 million. I was delighted.

Seth immediately brought me back down to earth. "I think we've got to let this play out." My question was concerning where it could go. Would I have taken that first offer right on the spot? Absolutely. But it wasn't going to go down, and I kind of wanted to see the process.

In Seth's conversations with Theo, he said it was all very professional, but that the Red Sox were suggesting that while they really liked me, they weren't moving off this offer. They also were implying that the third year was a concession on their part. My thinking, however, was that if they were going to three for $36 million, they could definitely go four for $48 million. Let's see if we can get that fourth year.

Now the deadline passed for the Red Sox's exclusive negotiating period, and other teams were allowed to get into the fray. Going into this area, the only caveat I reminded Seth of was, "Look, I don't mind opening the door, but let's backtrack three months. We were hoping for three at thirty million. We've surpassed that. Love and hate are emotions that go hand in hand, so just guarantee we don't reach the point where they pull the offer off the table. You can negotiate until the cows come home, but just make sure they don't pull the offer."

His answer: "They won't because they want you."

I had asked him that same question right before signing my first three-year deal with the Marlins, when they started at $5.7 million. Then, I hadn't made even a third of the .7 million in my life yet, so I was saying, "Sign it! Sign it!" He just said, "Hold on. I guarantee you they won't pull that deal off the table." A few days later I signed for $6.5 million.

Then my second deal came when the Marlins started at four years. There were other guys out there with worse stats who had better deals. But once again, I put my faith in Sam and Seth, and we ended up with a more favorable deal.

So here we were again, with me telling Seth to negotiate all he wanted but just make that same promise. But now the other teams were coming in, and then the hesitation started. It wasn't so much any kind of second-guessing concerning my desire to return to Boston, but rather simply wondering if the people who were making the decisions really wanted me back.

This I did know: Three teams—the Phillies, the Dodgers, and my old club, the Yankees—did want me, and they were ready to show exactly to what extent. The kid who couldn't crack varsity was now being chased with some of the biggest checkbooks in the game.

One of the first things I started looking at with all of these teams was where they played their home games. I knew Fenway was perfect for me, which factored in with how much I loved playing for Terry Francona and how the appreciation of the Boston fans still was giving me goose bumps.

But Philadelphia, which didn't become a player until their pitching situation settled in via the trade for Brad Lidge, seemed like a pretty solid place for me to call home. In eighteen games at Citizens Bank Park, I had hit a gaudy .353 with seven home runs. I looked at Philly as almost the same as Fenway without the high wall in left. I would be in the middle of Jimmy Rollins, Shane Victorino, Chase Utley, Ryan Howard, and Pat Burrell. And, besides the prospects of potentially having four huge years there, I also relished the idea of playing in Miami three times.

While I hadn't hit as well in Dodger Stadium, playing for a good team in Los Angeles was intriguing. LA also had come on strong, seemingly intent on making the best offer throughout the entirety of the process.

Early in my conversations with Sam and Seth a couple of other teams that piqued my interest were Atlanta and Detroit. In terms of the Braves, I had heard some rumors they were thinking of moving Chipper Jones from third base, and I never came across somebody saying a bad word about playing for Bobby Cox. And, once again, the proximity to my home in South Florida was appealing.

As far as Detroit, I thought that if they didn't pick up Ivan Rodriguez's option, Brandon Inge, their current third baseman, might go to catcher, and I have a special appreciation for their general manager, Dave Dombrowski. When we were together with the Marlins he was a guy who knew every aspect of the game, but never talked baseball with the players in the sense of saying something like, "Oh, you're too relaxed at the plate." It was just, "Are you feeling good? Good, keep going." He left the baseball stuff to the baseball people. I respected that more and more as I kept playing.

The Tigers' manager, Jim Leyland, is also my kind of guy. He doesn't care about ego, he gets in everyone's face, and I like that. There shouldn't be different treatment of players because of the numbers somebody puts up. Aren't we a team? We're all in there together. We're not all blessed with the same power, but we all can go on the same path.

Then there were the Yankees.

I had made it clear that even though I had lived through the Red Sox–Yankees rivalry for the past two years, my view of New York was still a bit different from those in the Sox clubhouse. This was the team I was born and bred on when it came to professional baseball, and many of those who were nurtured along with me were still wearing pinstripes.

When Yankees owner George Steinbrenner came up to me as a minor leaguer and said, "You keep doing what you're doing and you're going to wear pinstripes a long time," that was powerful stuff.

But there were three problems when it came to the

situation with the Yanks. First was the park. As much as Fenway is tailored to my swing, Yankee Stadium is the polar opposite. Sure, I had hit a respectable .278 there in 22 games, but only saw 3 home runs go over a left-field wall that succumbs to a whole lot of outfield in front of it. The one thing I didn't want to do was sign a deal and not be able to live up to the numbers.

The second issue was the return of Alex Rodriguez, my double-play partner on the Christopher Columbus High junior-varsity team back in Miami. After his agent, Scott Boras, announced that Alex would be opting out of his Yankees contract at basically the same time I was celebrating my home run off Aaron Cook, Rodriguez changed his course of action. A-Rod made peace with the Yankees and agreed to a new deal to return as the team's third baseman. And while I wouldn't mind playing first base at some point in my career, the prospects of manning that spot now, as New York was suggesting, wasn't really an option.

Finally, I couldn't forget the fans.

I remember my first day in the big leagues was in Boston. Ricky Ledee and I took a cab from the airport to the hotel and there were sixty Yankee fans outside waiting. We got out and everybody started shouting, "Mike!" and "Ricky!" I couldn't fathom that they knew who we were. That's when I realized the passion that came with being a follower of the Yankees. That said, there was never a true connection with those people. How could there be? I played in eight games and basically pinch-hit. How could there be any kind of connection?

My relationship with the followers of the Red Sox, well, that was another story.

While the Yankees organization did hold a special place in my heart, it was no match for the spot reserved for the baseball fans of New England. Truth be told, I could have never gone and played for the Yankees after everything that happened with the Red Sox in '07. We won the World Series and I was the World Series MVP, and that next year I was going to New York? I believed that if that happened everything I did would be thrown away because of one thing, and I didn't want that to happen. I'm sure Yankees fans make their players feel appreciated, but they were never going to make me feel as wanted as the Red Sox fans had over the last two years.

So, with a week to go before the day the Red Sox mandated as the deadline to take their offer, I told my agents words that made them cringe: "You can continue bluffing all you want, but I'm playing in Boston. If they don't move another dollar, I'm still going to take the three for thirty-six million dollars." That wasn't what Sam and Seth wanted to hear.

The Red Sox were going on the premise that there is a drop-off when a player hits thirty-five, but that was a tough sell in my eyes. I understood their reasoning, but I don't consider myself part of the norm, and haven't my whole life. That's where I really believe you have to take it on a case-by-case basis.

The other aspect of the negotiations that was really starting to wear on me was the unbalanced level of adoration on behalf of the Red Sox and my other suitors. Here were all these teams that I hadn't played a game for telling me, "We're going to give you this, and give you that." It's basically like you're being recruited. You're the hotshot college recruit who walks into the stadium and is greeted by your image up on the Jumbotron with the announcer bellowing your name—except in this case the place you really want to go has the biggest and best video screen and sound system but turns it off the minute you walk onto the field. It's part of negotiations—this I understood. But it was still a tough pill to swallow.

Talking to Bertica really helped me put it in perspective. I told her that a part of me really wanted those four years because I didn't know how long I was going to play. But she helped remind me how much I liked the city of Boston, and didn't want to learn a whole new city. Why ruin a good thing? I had already made plenty of money, and after going through a season like '05, with everyone saying how my career was coming to an end, I understood how fickle this world could be. If things go bad I have no problem walking away from the game. I made my money, no problem.

But while everybody says it's not about the money, that's only true some of the time. I know from experience that when you've made money it's a lot easier to say it's not about the money.

My first deal? That was all about the money. They offered me $5 million. For everything my dad has done, he will still never make $5 million, so that put it in perspective for me. And then I started thinking how teammates go other places and they're not as happy because they took the extra year or the extra dollars. Could I look my father in the face and say, "I'm really unhappy because I'm making $13 million over the next four years"? He would punch me through the wall, because what I would make over three years it would take him 280 years to get.

With all of that in mind I knew this time I was going to go where I was happy. It was almost a no-brainer, but I had also never been a free agent and wanted to take it slow. I didn't want there to be any tricks or sign something like Bronson Arroyo did when he ended up with another team almost before the ink dried on his extension.

The whole process was kind of unappetizing. It's not personal, but it really is personal in some ways. It's a business, but in another light it isn't a business. I tried to put myself in their shoes, but it was hard.

During the negotiations I did talk to our general manager, Theo Epstein, once, and our principal owner, John Henry, about three times (once while on the Peter Pan ride at Disney World's Magic Kingdom). It wasn't like they were calling me out of the blue. Everything was cleared with Sam and Seth. When Theo called I felt like maybe they were trying to break me down a little bit, trying to find out if I was intent on sticking to my guns or if I was really a little bit soft. That's when I put my business face on.

When Mr. Henry called I simply told him, "I'm an open book. I want to play for your team. And I don't have a problem taking a discount. But the market is definitely over thirteen million dollars and we're stuck at thirty-seven million for three years. And those other teams are offering me no-trade clauses and all kinds of perks I'm not getting from you guys.

"Mr. Henry, I look at two things. After 2005 you guys made an eighteen-million-dollar gamble on me to acquire Josh Beckett. Now, I'm not dumb. You signed J. T. Snow, and Kevin Youkilis was on the team in case I had the same season I had in '05. You would have swallowed the eighteen million, played Youk at third, and played J. T. Snow at first. And you know what? I'm happy it worked out for you, and I'm happy it worked out for me. But it was still an eighteen-million-dollar gamble. Now you're asking me to leave upward of eighteen million dollars on the table. So you're asking me to take the same eighteen-million-dollar gamble. You know what? I'll concede that. But I need you to understand that conceding the fourth year is a major concession. In the business world, when you give up something, you get something. There's a premium. You don't just give up things because of the goodness of your heart."

I went on to tell him that I was really struggling with all these teams who didn't know me and were going solely on reputation. They were bending over backward to get me, and the Red Sox wanted to even front-load the original proposal, which would have made me even more tradable than ever.

"There might be only one team in the big leagues that generates more revenue than you guys, and I'm thinking the difference between what we have in getting this done is just six hundred fifty thousand dollars a year," I continued. "You're not giving me a no-trade. I'm conceding I'm taking well below market value, and all we're apart is six hundred fifty thousand a year. You guys probably sell six hundred fifty thousand dollars' worth of hot dogs in about five innings. You made an eighteen-million-dollar gamble, you asked me to leave eighteen million on the table, and here we have a difference of six hundred fifty thousand a year?"

I would talk to Mr. Henry one more time, the night before the Red Sox–imposed deadline to take or leave their offer. Boston had imposed a one p.m. jumping-off point on Monday afternoon, and I told John, "Mr. Henry, if the deal stays where it is right now, the deadline doesn't mean anything." I immediately turned around and told Seth that if they want to put a one p.m. deadline on the deal, then tell them it has to be three p.m. and then have them give me their final offer, because then I will know where they stand. If they don't want to budge at all, then we would really start talking to the other teams.

The night before the deadline things got interesting again with Ruben Amaro, the Phillies' assistant general manager, calling Seth to see if he could talk to me, which I had no problem with. So Ruben called and he started telling me how they really want a right-handed bat that could produce runs hitting after two of the National League's best hitters, Chase Utley and Ryan Howard. I started hearing all of this, began to think about the park again, and started to count the number of runs I could potentially drive in. Needless to say, the phone conversation had a really good vibe to it and really made me rethink some things.

I finished by telling Ruben that if he wanted to talk about

money or length he was going to have to deal with Seth, and that I still should touch base with the Phillies' manager, Charlie Manuel, because at the end of the day that's the guy I deal with. I mean, guys like John Henry and the Red Sox president, Larry Lucchino, I see about four times a year, but Terry Francona I get to beat in cribbage every day. So I got in touch with Charlie.

"Mike, we like to win and we play hard," Manuel said. Playing against them the last few years, I could see that. I liked their style, taking the extra bag and staying aggressive. It didn't hurt that I was a huge Phillies fan growing up. Our family had made a trip to Philadelphia when I was six years old and we went to Burger King. I ordered a Kid's Meal, which included three baseball cards, one of which was Mike Schmidt, who was identified as a National League All-Star. I asked my dad, "Is this guy good?" He told me Schmidt was really good.

When we got back from Philly, Dad taught me how to read a box score. So every morning I would wake up, grab a newspaper, and start dissecting the box scores from the night before. That year, 1980, Schmidt won the MVP and the Phillies won the World Series. I was sold.

The Phillies were offering a lot more, and they were doing it solely on reputation. I hadn't driven in a run for them. And imagine if we won the whole thing, which they hadn't done since 1980. Now you have three cities where you were playing a major part of making history. It all started getting in my head a little bit. I told them we would call back.

But there were certain things I still couldn't shake, most

of which were all things that came with the situation in Boston. My family liked the city, and the fans were a major factor, but what remained as the biggest drawing card was undoubtedly my teammates and manager. That's another reason why the Yankees thing wasn't as attractive. I would join New York and then I was supposed to hate these guys on the Red Sox? I'm supposed to want to crush them? That didn't fit with me.

All along the negotiating process I was receiving text messages from teammates, but, as I told Seth, you don't know who these messages are coming from. My teammates are solid, but let's just say I tell Dustin Pedroia, "Dude, we're just bluffing, man. I'm going to stay with Boston." Then Francona is going to call him and ask him if he knows what's going on, and Petie is going to tell him, "Don't tell anybody, but he's just bluffing." I didn't want to put those people in that situation. But the fact that they were interested made me feel good.

Alex Cora, for instance, texted me the night the Red Sox were going to lose exclusive negotiating rights, asking, "Are we still teammates?" I sent something back saying, "I don't know about teammates, but we're still friends." And, as it turned out, it was those sorts of friends who allowed me to remain their teammates, as well.

About eleven p.m. Sunday night, after talking with the Phillies and reflecting on the situation with the Red Sox, I was about to go to bed, and Seth called me. They said the Red Sox had come up another $500,000, to $37.5 million.

"You know what?" I said to Seth. "This is never going to turn into forty, forty-two, or forty-five, and if it did, it would be with the other teams. I don't want to go back and forth any-more. The deal's done. If you want to work out something else, go ahead. But I'm going to go with those numbers." And, true to form, Seth went back in, talked with Theo into the early-morning hours, and did come away with something more than just my accepted dollar amounts. He got me a hotel suite on every road trip. When he told me that, I was almost more ex-cited about the suite than the $37.5 million.

When I got up at six a.m. the next morning to take my kids to school, I was happy. Happy with the way we approached things, happy that I was staying in Boston, and happy my hotel rooms were going to be appreciably more spacious for the next three seasons.

The way I looked at it was if the next free-agent third baseman signs for $70 million, I won't be upset because I didn't make any money before.

Like Dad said to his eight-year-old Little League hero, "You have to want to be the guy that's in that situation—because a lot of people say they want to be in that situation, but they don't want to be in that situation."

A few months after signing, I received one of the first perks from my new lot in life. I gave a postgame pep talk to a basket-ball team in Spokane, Washington.

Mike Redmond had invited me to attend a Gonzaga men's basketball game during my family's New Year's trip to visit his brood in Washington. Red was one of the school's most nota-ble alumni, along with the former NBA star John Stockton, and he garnered a lot of respect on campus. The plan was to check out the New Year's Day game with Mike, and then go back to his house for a big party. Of course, the event would include seats right behind the Gonzaga bench. *The* Mike Redmond wouldn't have it any other way. Midway through the first half the public-address announcer said, "We have a very special announcement. Gonzaga's own Mike Redmond is here in attendance. And a very good friend of his is also in attendance, World Series MVP Mike Lowell." When I was holding that MVP trophy back on Coors Field, I never thought that months later I'd be singled out at a Gonzaga hoop game, but it was a nice gesture.

After soaking in the whole college atmosphere, along with the Gonzaga victory, we were both invited back in the home team's locker room after the game. I asked Mike, the big man on campus, if he was going to say something to the team. "I don't think so," he demurred. "Well, I'm here. I might as well say something to these guys," I shot back. Considering Red had delivered with our playoff credo ("Push, push, push, grind, grind, grind" was still lingering in my psyche months after the final out in Colorado), offering something back to his alma mater was the least I could do.

As I stared at this collection of kids, I could see a lot of myself in them. They were young, and some were hungry, but others were going through the motions. You can sense the different personalities that come with any team. Asking their coach, Mark Few, if I could say a few words wasn't at all awkward. If my initial motivation for the speech was to help out

Red, now my priority was to help these kids in any way I could.

I told the group how much I enjoyed watching them play. And then I went on to let them know the importance of selling out to your program, and selling out to yourself. Whether you're in school, whether you're running sprints, you never know when your opportunity is going to end. Then I pointed to Red and said, "Look at Mike here. Look at that body. If that body could make it to the big leagues for ten years, anyone can do it." Well, Mike wasn't going to let me have all the fun.

"I'm going to say something, too," Red jumped in, suddenly getting all riled up. I had used terms like "sell out" when I really wanted to say something to the effect of "I don't give a shit about what anyone tells you you can or can't do." But I thought, this being a Catholic school and all, I really should use the clean version. Mike, the heralded Gonzaga grad, set me straight.

"You know, look at me. I ain't shit," exclaimed Red, his face suddenly flushed with color. "But I'll tell you what. I fucking laid it on the line every time I had to because I didn't know when I might have this opportunity again." Our messages weren't all that different, other than the fact that he cursed at least eight times in about two minutes. Mike never got like that, and that's why I think the message of what he was saying truly sunk in.

I also think we both believed what we preached. Here was Mike, an undrafted free agent, with me, a twentieth-rounder, both trying to summarize our struggles in a matter of a couple of minutes. Six hundred guys were drafted in front of me. Six hundred! That means the scouts thought that six hundred guys had a better chance of making it to the big leagues than I did. And I'm willing to bet that not one of those six hundred guys got to give a postgame pep talk to the Gonzaga men's basketball team.

There I was, in the middle of a bunch of college kids, surrounded by the first snowfall my kids had ever seen, while witnessing Mike Redmond deliver one of the most surreal motivational speeches I had ever heard. I was officially living the life of a world champion.

Despite all the twists and turns, smiles and frowns, and constant stream of reality checks—there was nowhere I would rather be.

Acknowledgments

As much as this book is my story, it would have never been possible if not for my writer, Rob Bradford. Thank you, Rob, for putting my life into words that I can share with others. I can't tell you how much I appreciate your tireless work, through holidays and weekends, and your sacrificing family time for our project. Your professionalism is second to none.

But as thorough a job as Rob did, of course there is no way that he could uncover every detail in my life, and that is something I would neither expect nor desire. That said, sometimes we must recognize the details. And in that spirit, I would like to take this opportunity to thank those who may not have been mentioned in the book but have had a profound impact on everything I have been able to accomplish, overcome, attain, enjoy, celebrate, and realize.

To my mom, Beatriz: Over the course of my long journey to this surreal, male-dominated life of big-league baseball, it seems like you have been the silent partner. I am amazed at how you handled endless car drop-offs to all of my sporting games, practices, and events. I know at times they seemed endless. The way you always encouraged us children to strive for the better, the way you treated us all equally, and taught us the importance of faith, family, and education—for all of this I thank you. And on top of all those "duties," I can honestly say our daily home-cooked dinners as a family were a testament to your undeniable talents and love. For that I am forever indebted.

From here I will start with my elementary school P.E. teacher, Ron Ziccardi. Thanks for showing young kids the value in teams and sports and for your nonstop enthusiasm as you coached us. The love I have, especially for the sport of basketball, was instilled in me by you and I can never forget how much we looked forward to the "Express" coming into town.

To my baseball coaches at Gables Senior High, Dave Bisceglia and Orlando Castro: Thanks for putting a value on the mental aspect of baseball and bringing back the love for a game that I had lost. You both were the foundation of a great revival of confidence in a skinny fifteen-year-old who just wanted to enjoy the game. My summer experiences are unforgettable with "BP off Stro."

As an intimidated eleventh-grader entering a new environment of four thousand students, I was grateful for the self-less support and sheer friendship of Tom Peck, Ross Atkins, and Ron Yacoub. Our paths crossed at the Little League level and started a bond of accomplishment. Ross, hopefully when you are a GM, I can work for you someday. To Marc Rodriguez and

Bobby Beyra, thank you for the endless rides home from practice, because without your generosity I would have felt stuck.

An extreme thank-you, however, belongs to Ralph Masso and Juany Alvarez. Uncertainty surrounds most changes in life, and in high school I found out the true meaning of old-school friendship . . . strong, loyal, and unconditional. It is my honor to have you as my friends, and never vice versa. Now, I know friends were mentioned throughout the book, but a personal note must be added to the names Garo Friguls, Andy Fernandez, Leo Leon, Alex Garcia, Eddy Garcia, Joche Espin, and Ron Yacoub. Most people are lucky to have one childhood friend who ends up being a lifelong friend. But to grow up with guys who are your best friends since the age of six, and about thirty years later have it remain the same, is just unbelievable. Not a hitch, hiccup, or bump. I am spoiled because I feel like I was raised not only with two great brothers but with eight. May the Lord bless us with many more BBQs, vacations, poker nights, and fishing trips together. Although you came in a little later, George Pino, you are in immediately if not sooner.

When I entered college, more things were learned and relationships established, but some definitely stand out more than others—Jimmy Hopler and Kevin Wehn, to be exact. Opening your doors to a new freshman, especially in the mornings after mandatory weights, meant the world. Hoppy, you taught me what it really meant to work in the gym, never going through the motions and pushing those weights, or "pillows," as you would call them. An upperclassman in you, Kevin, giving me total support, showed what a stand-up guy you were from day

one. To my eventual roommate Eddie Ferrer, thanks for bringing back—along with Francisco Lebron—a piece of my Puerto
Rican culture. I was told by my father that in his experiences
Puerto Rican friends are the most loyal, and Eddie, you are the
poster boy for that. To my coach Danny Price, thanks for
putting your faith in a freshman to produce right away when
even he didn't know he was capable.

There were also times when pure acts of kindness made
me realize the good in the world, even though the media
seems to harp on negativity. This I saw firsthand in the minor
leagues, and for that I would like to thank Tony Latour and
Andy Feltz. Tony, giving me rent-free lodging during my Instructional League days in Tampa sure helped me focus solely
on baseball and further my development. Andy, allowing me
to stay in Manhattan as a September call-up allowed my first
big-league experience to be truly unforgettable. Your never
wanting anything in return once I "made it" showed a true
example of what friendship and family are all about.

As my professional life continued, my friendships with Jason
Troilo and Carlos Yedo were further established. Can't find two
better people to grind it out with than you guys. Teammates can
come and go but friendships like ours remain strong.

When I finally embarked on my big-league career, I had to
find representation. Here is where Sam and Seth Levinson
stepped in. I received unwavering support in good times and
tough times and felt privileged to find people who cared not
only about the business but the family. I thank you for not
only your honesty and guidance but your flexibility in allowing

me to make my decisions. Thanks for not only steering my career in the right direction but becoming close friends.

Much like with the Levinsons, this next friendship started as business. To Gaspar Contreras, thanks for your attention to detail and mental focus on our off-season boxing workouts. I truly believe they were instrumental in helping me through my greatest professional year of 2007.

Speaking of close friends, I must now change gears to one of my wife's: Ana Suarez. Thank you for not only allowing us to use your office for some marathon sessions in creating this book, but for the change you brought out in my wife. Circumstances left a sour taste of friendship for my wife, but you came along at just the right time, and I truly believe you healed her soul and made her heart whole. You are always looked upon as family.

As far as family goes, I have been blessed with one that is solid and united in all areas. They say godparents should be an extension of your real parents, and mine absolutely are. I can't tell you, Aunty Baby and Tio Gerardo, how much I enjoyed looking in the crowd and seeing you two there with unwavering support from Little League to the big stage.

As in everyone's life we feel that some of those who have touched us left us a little too early. To Grandma, you always said you thought I could accomplish great things, and it was you I pointed to after the final out of game six of the 2003 World Series. Thanks for looking out for me from above. To Papito, thanks for endless tennis and golf outings. I don't need pictures to recall these memories because they are etched in my soul. May you both continue to rest in peace and may God bless you.

Family is important but one thing is true. We don't choose them. You don't choose your parents, your brothers or sisters, or your kids. But you do choose your spouse. To my wonderful Bertica, thanks for being the mother you are, the friend you are, and the rock that has never wavered from my side. I don't know what the future holds, but knowing it is with you always brings a smile to my face. I love you.

Thanks should also go out to the literary agent Barbara Collins Rosenberg, whose guidance through the process was truly invaluable. Also, I am appreciative of all the hard work and expertise our editor, Mark Chait, put into the project. Both Barbara and Mark did an unbelievable job in helping make the process work. Thanks, also, to Raymond Garcia at Celebra.

The last acknowledgment does not go to a friend, family member, or coach. This one goes to a game. The game of baseball. I have wanted to excel at this game since the age of six, and countless hours of blood, sweat, and, yes, even tears have come my way in order to do so. Yet I can honestly say it has never been work. There is no better feeling in the professional world than being on a baseball field. There I find peace, freedom, and absolute joy. This sport has been involved in my life's biggest challenges and also in some of my greatest triumphs. Performing at a high level on hallowed grounds like Fenway Park in front of its fans is just one of those joys I have been blessed with. May God continue to give me the strength to maximize my talents to bring honor to this great game that nourishes my soul and keeps allowing me to look forward to the next game with childlike enthusiasm.

To everyone who reads this, thanks for sharing in my ride.